The Ancestry Detective:
A Beginner's Guide to Uncovering Your Family History

Charles Pembroke

Charles Pembroke

The Ancestry Detective

Dedicated to Christine Rosaline Barker

Charles Pembroke

© Copyright 2025 - All rights reserved.

The content contained within this book may not be reproduced, duplicated or transmitted without direct written permission from Charles Pembroke or PAB Publications.

Under no circumstances will any blame or legal responsibility be held against the publisher, or author, for any damages, reparation, or monetary loss due to the information contained within this book, either directly or indirectly.

Legal Notice:

This book is copyright-protected. It is only for personal use. You cannot amend, distribute, sell, use, quote or paraphrase any part, or the content within this book, without the consent of the author or publisher.

Disclaimer Notice:

Please note the information contained within this document is for educational and entertainment purposes only. All effort has been executed to present accurate, up to date, reliable, complete information. No warranties of any kind are declared or implied. Readers acknowledge that the author is not engaged in the rendering of legal, financial, medical or professional advice. The content within this book has been derived from various sources. Please consult a licensed professional before attempting any techniques outlined in this book.

By reading this document, the reader agrees that under no circumstances is the author responsible for any losses, direct or indirect, that are incurred as a result of the use of the information contained within this document, including, but not limited to, errors, omissions, or inaccuracies.

The Ancestry Detective

CHAPTER 1: BECOMING AN ANCESTRY DETECTIVE: YOUR FIRST STEPS — 1

WELCOME TO THE JOURNEY: WHY EXPLORE YOUR FAMILY HISTORY? — 1
SETTING YOUR GOALS: WHAT DO YOU HOPE TO DISCOVER? — 3
THE DETECTIVE'S MINDSET: PRINCIPLES OF GENEALOGICAL RESEARCH — 5
ESSENTIAL TOOLS OF THE TRADE: NOTEBOOKS, SOFTWARE, AND ONLINE ACCOUNTS — 9
BEGINNING YOUR RESEARCH LOG: WHY DOCUMENTATION IS CRUCIAL — 11
UNDERSTANDING PRIVACY AND ETHICS: RESEARCHING LIVING RELATIVES — 14
AVOIDING COMMON PITFALLS: SURNAME MYTHS, BRICK WALLS, AND ONLINE RUMORS — 17
GETTING ORGANIZED FROM THE START: CREATING A DEDICATED WORKSPACE — 20
BUILDING YOUR FOUNDATION: THE INITIAL PEDIGREE CHART AND FAMILY GROUP SHEETS — 22
LOOKING AHEAD: WHAT THIS BOOK WILL HELP YOU ACHIEVE — 25

CHAPTER 2: STARTING WITH THE KNOWN: INTERVIEWING YOUR RELATIVES — 27

THE RICHEST SOURCE: WHY LIVING RELATIVES ARE INVALUABLE — 27
PLANNING YOUR INTERVIEWS: IDENTIFYING KEY RELATIVES AND PREPARING QUESTIONS — 30
CONDUCTING THE INTERVIEW: TECHNIQUES FOR ELICITING INFORMATION AND BUILDING RAPPORT — 34
RECORDING THE CONVERSATION: AUDIO, VIDEO, AND NOTE-TAKING — 37
BEYOND THE FACTS: ELICITING STORIES, MEMORIES, AND FAMILY LORE — 41

THE POWER OF SHOW AND TELL: ASKING ABOUT PHOTOS, DOCUMENTS, AND ARTIFACTS — 44
INTERVIEWING DIFFERENT GENERATIONS: TAILORING YOUR APPROACH — 47
HANDLING DIFFICULT OR SENSITIVE TOPICS: NAVIGATING FAMILY SECRETS AND TRAUMA — 50
FOLLOWING UP AND SHARING: KEEPING RELATIVES ENGAGED — 53
THE INFORMATION HARVEST: SYNTHESIZING INTERVIEW DATA AND IDENTIFYING CLUES — 55

CHAPTER 3: ORGANIZING YOUR ANCESTRAL ARCHIVES: TAMING THE PAPER TRAIL — 59

THE IMPORTANCE OF ORGANIZATION: PREVENTING CHAOS AND ENSURING PROGRESS — 59
PHYSICAL ORGANIZATION SYSTEMS: FILES, BINDERS, AND STORAGE SOLUTIONS — 62
DIGITAL ORGANIZATION SYSTEMS: FOLDERS, NAMING CONVENTIONS, AND CLOUD STORAGE — 67
MANAGING YOUR RESEARCH LOG: DETAILED TRACKING OF SEARCHES AND RESULTS — 71
SOURCE CITATIONS MADE SIMPLE: WHY AND HOW TO CITE YOUR INFORMATION — 74
HOW TO CITE YOUR SOURCES (THE SIMPLE APPROACH FOR BEGINNERS): — 75
EVALUATING YOUR SOURCES: THE GENEALOGICAL PROOF STANDARD — 77
APPLYING THE PRINCIPLES OF EVALUATION AS A BEGINNER: — 79
HANDLING DIFFERENT DOCUMENT TYPES: CERTIFICATES, LETTERS, PHOTOS, AND MORE — 80
BACKING UP YOUR DATA: PROTECTING YOUR PRECIOUS RESEARCH — 84
INTEGRATING INTERVIEWS AND DOCUMENTS: CONNECTING STORIES WITH RECORDS — 87

REVIEWING AND REFINING YOUR SYSTEM: ADAPTING YOUR
ORGANIZATION AS YOU PROGRESS 89

CHAPTER 4: NAVIGATING THE DIGITAL LANDSCAPE: ESSENTIAL ONLINE RESOURCES 93

THE INTERNET: A GENEALOGIST'S GOLDMINE 93
MAJOR GENEALOGY PLATFORMS: ANCESTRY, FAMILYSEARCH, FINDMYPAST, MYHERITAGE 96
CHOOSING THE RIGHT PLATFORM(S): 99
EXPLORING FREE DATABASES AND WEBSITES: A WEALTH OF ACCESSIBLE INFORMATION 100
UNDERSTANDING DIGITIZED RECORDS: WHAT'S AVAILABLE AND HOW TO ACCESS IT 102
WORKING WITH DIGITIZED RECORDS: 104
UTILIZING ONLINE TREES AND USER-SUBMITTED INFORMATION: PROMISES AND PERILS 106
UTILIZING ONLINE TREES EFFECTIVELY AND ETHICALLY: 108
BEYOND THE BIG NAMES: EXPLORING ARCHIVAL WEBSITES, LIBRARY CATALOGS, AND HISTORICAL SOCIETIES ONLINE 109
TIPS FOR EXPLORING THESE RESOURCES: 112
EFFECTIVE SEARCHING TECHNIQUES: KEYWORDS, WILDCARDS, AND FILTERING RESULTS 113
ONLINE COMMUNITIES AND FORUMS: CONNECTING WITH OTHER RESEARCHERS 119
BENEFITS OF ENGAGING WITH ONLINE COMMUNITIES: 120
STAYING UP-TO-DATE: FOLLOWING GENEALOGY BLOGS, PODCASTS, AND NEWSLETTERS 122

CHAPTER 5: DECODING VITAL RECORDS: BIRTHS, MARRIAGES, AND DEATHS 125

THE CORNERSTONES OF GENEALOGY: WHY VITAL RECORDS ARE CRUCIAL 125
BIRTH RECORDS: INFORMATION ON INDIVIDUALS AND PARENTS 128

FINDING AND USING BIRTH RECORDS: 129
MARRIAGE RECORDS: PROOF OF UNION AND CLUES TO FAMILY CONNECTIONS 132
FINDING AND USING MARRIAGE RECORDS: 134
TIPS FOR USING MARRIAGE RECORDS: 135
DEATH RECORDS: CONFIRMING PASSING AND REVEALING KEY DETAILS 136
TIPS FOR USING DEATH RECORDS: 139
ACCESSING VITAL RECORDS: STATE, COUNTY, AND LOCAL ARCHIVES 140
ACCESSING RECORDS IN PERSON: 143
REQUESTING RECORDS BY MAIL OR ONLINE: PROCEDURES AND TIPS FOR SUCCESS 144
UNDERSTANDING HISTORICAL VARIATIONS: HOW VITAL RECORDS HAVE CHANGED OVER TIME 147
INTERPRETING THE INFORMATION: DECIPHERING HANDWRITING, ABBREVIATIONS, AND JARGON 150
BEYOND THE CERTIFICATE: USING VITAL RECORDS AS SPRINGBOARDS FOR FURTHER RESEARCH 154
TROUBLESHOOTING MISSING RECORDS: ALTERNATIVE SOURCES WHEN VITAL RECORDS ARE UNAVAILABLE 156

CHAPTER 6: UNLOCKING STORIES IN THE CENSUS: A SNAPSHOT OF THE PAST 161

MORE THAN JUST NAMES: THE RICH INFORMATION IN CENSUS RECORDS 161
THE EVOLUTION OF THE CENSUS: CHANGES IN QUESTIONS AND COVERAGE OVER TIME 164
ACCESSING CENSUS RECORDS: ONLINE DATABASES AND MICROFILM 169
SEARCHING STRATEGIES FOR CENSUS RECORDS: NAME VARIATIONS, LOCATION, AND NEIGHBORS 171
INTERPRETING CENSUS DATA: UNDERSTANDING COLUMNS, ABBREVIATIONS, AND ENUMERATOR PRACTICES 174

The Ancestry Detective

BEYOND YOUR DIRECT LINE: USING CENSUS RECORDS TO TRACE EXTENDED FAMILY — 177
MAPPING YOUR ANCESTORS: USING CENSUS DATA TO UNDERSTAND NEIGHBORHOODS AND COMMUNITIES — 180
IDENTIFYING CLUES FOR FURTHER RESEARCH: OCCUPATIONS, BIRTHPLACES, AND OTHER HINTS — 182
DEALING WITH MISSING OR DAMAGED CENSUS RECORDS: ALTERNATIVE SOURCES — 184
CENSUS SECRETS AND STORIES: WHAT YOU CAN LEARN ABOUT YOUR ANCESTORS' LIVES — 186

CHAPTER 7: INVESTIGATING IMMIGRATION AND MIGRATION: TRACING ANCESTORS' MOVEMENTS — 191

THE MIGRATORY URGE: UNDERSTANDING HISTORICAL PATTERNS OF MOVEMENT — 192
IMMIGRATION RECORDS: PASSENGER LISTS AND BORDER CROSSINGS — 194
PORT OF ENTRY RESEARCH: EXPLORING MAJOR PORTS AND THEIR RECORDS — 198
NATURALIZATION RECORDS: BECOMING A CITIZEN — 201
INTERNAL MIGRATION: MOVING WITHIN A COUNTRY — 204
SOURCES FOR TRACKING INTERNAL MIGRATION: DEEDS, TAX RECORDS, AND LOCAL HISTORIES — 206
UNDERSTANDING PUSH AND PULL FACTORS: WHY DID YOUR ANCESTORS MOVE? — 209
MAPPING MIGRATION ROUTES: VISUALIZING YOUR ANCESTORS' JOURNEYS — 210
CASE STUDIES IN MIGRATION: FOLLOWING FAMILIES ACROSS CONTINENTS AND COUNTRIES — 212
THE IMPACT OF MIGRATION ON FAMILY: HOW MOVING SHAPED YOUR ANCESTORS' LIVES — 213

CHAPTER 8: DISCOVERING MILITARY RECORDS: FINDING INFORMATION IN SERVICE RECORDS — 217

BEYOND THE BATTLEFIELD: THE VALUE OF MILITARY RECORDS FOR GENEALOGISTS	218
IDENTIFYING MILITARY ANCESTORS: STARTING WITH FAMILY STORIES AND BASIC RECORDS	221
EXPLORING DIFFERENT CONFLICTS AND SERVICE PERIODS: RECORDS BY ERA AND BRANCH	223
ACCESSING MILITARY RECORDS: NATIONAL ARCHIVES, ONLINE DATABASES, AND VETERANS' ORGANIZATIONS	226
INTERPRETING MILITARY DOCUMENTS: UNDERSTANDING TERMINOLOGY AND FORMS	229
PENSION RECORDS: A WEALTH OF FAMILY INFORMATION	232
DRAFT RECORDS AND ENROLLMENT LISTS: IDENTIFYING POTENTIAL SERVICE	234
RECORDS OF MILITARY UNITS: TRACING YOUR ANCESTOR'S COMPANY OR SHIP	237
MILITARY CEMETERIES AND BURIAL RECORDS: LOCATING FINAL RESTING PLACES	239
CONNECTING WITH MILITARY HISTORY: UNDERSTANDING THE CONTEXT OF YOUR ANCESTOR'S SERVICE	241

CHAPTER 9: UNLOCKING LAND AND PROPERTY RECORDS: USING DEEDS AND OTHER LAND DOCUMENTS 243

BEYOND OWNERSHIP: HOW LAND RECORDS REVEAL FAMILY CONNECTIONS AND MOVEMENTS	244
TYPES OF LAND RECORDS: DEEDS, MORTGAGES, GRANTS, AND PATENTS	247
ACCESSING LAND RECORDS: COUNTY COURTHOUSES AND ONLINE RESOURCES	250
UNDERSTANDING LEGAL DESCRIPTIONS: METES AND BOUNDS, TOWNSHIP AND RANGE	253
GRANTOR AND GRANTEE INDEXES: NAVIGATING LAND RECORDS EFFECTIVELY	257

DEEDS AS GENEALOGICAL GOLDMINES: IDENTIFYING
RELATIONSHIPS, NEIGHBORS, AND MIGRATION CLUES   259
TAX RECORDS: TRACKING ANCESTORS THROUGH PROPERTY
ASSESSMENTS   261
PROBATE AND LAND: CONNECTING ESTATE SETTLEMENTS WITH
PROPERTY DIVISION   263
MAPPING YOUR ANCESTORS' LAND: VISUALIZING THEIR HOLDINGS
AND THEIR NEIGHBORS   265
CASE STUDIES IN LAND RESEARCH: SOLVING GENEALOGICAL
PUZZLES WITH PROPERTY RECORDS   266

CHAPTER 10: EXPLORING PROBATE AND COURT RECORDS: WILLS, ADMINISTRATIONS, AND LEGAL PROCEEDINGS — 269

BEYOND THE WILL: THE GENEALOGICAL RICHES IN PROBATE FILES
                                                    270
WILLS: IDENTIFYING HEIRS AND FAMILY RELATIONSHIPS   273
ADMINISTRATIONS: WHEN SOMEONE DIED WITHOUT A WILL   276
PROBATE INVENTORIES AND ACCOUNTS: GLIMPSES INTO
ANCESTORS' POSSESSIONS AND LIVES   278
GUARDIANSHIPS: RECORDS OF MINOR CHILDREN   281
ACCESSING PROBATE RECORDS: COUNTY COURTHOUSES AND
ARCHIVAL REPOSITORIES   283
UNDERSTANDING LEGAL TERMINOLOGY: DECIPHERING THE
LANGUAGE OF COURT DOCUMENTS   286
COURT RECORDS BEYOND PROBATE: LAWSUITS, CRIMINAL
PROCEEDINGS, AND OTHER ACTIONS   289
USING COURT RECORDS TO PROVE RELATIONSHIPS AND SOLVE
PROBLEMS   292
CASE STUDIES IN COURT RECORDS: UNLOCKING DIFFICULT
ANCESTRAL CONNECTIONS   295

CHAPTER 11: LEVERAGING DNA TESTING: UNDERSTANDING AND USING GENETIC GENEALOGY — 297

The Genetic Revolution: Incorporating DNA into Your Research 298
Types of DNA Tests: Autosomal, Y-DNA, and mtDNA 300
Choosing a DNA Testing Company: Comparing Services and Databases 304
Understanding Your Results: Ethnicity Estimates and DNA Matches 308
Working with DNA Matches: Identifying Common Ancestors and Confirming Relationships 310
Using Third-Party Tools: Enhancing Your DNA Analysis 313
Building and Using a Shared Matches Matrix: Visualizing DNA Connections 315
Applying DNA to Solve Genealogical Puzzles: Breaking Down Brick Walls 317
The Ethics of DNA Testing: Privacy, Unexpected Discoveries, and Informed Consent 320
Integrating DNA Findings with Documentary Evidence: Building a More Complete Picture 323

CHAPTER 12: WEAVING THE NARRATIVE: WRITING AND SHARING YOUR FAMILY STORY 327

Beyond the Names and Dates: Why Telling the Story Matters 328
Structuring Your Family History: Chronological, Topical, or Individual Stories 330
Bringing Ancestors to Life: Adding Historical Context and Detail 333
Writing Techniques for Genealogists: Crafting Engaging Prose 336
Including Visuals: Incorporating Photos, Documents, and Maps 338
Citing Sources in Your Writing: Giving Credit and Enabling Verification 341

CHOOSING YOUR MEDIUM: BOOKS, WEBSITES, BLOGS, AND PRESENTATIONS	**345**
PUBLISHING AND SHARING YOUR WORK: OPTIONS FOR DISTRIBUTION	**348**
PRESERVING YOUR RESEARCH FOR FUTURE GENERATIONS: ARCHIVING YOUR FINDINGS	**350**
THE ONGOING JOURNEY: CONTINUING YOUR ANCESTRY ADVENTURES	**352**

Charles Pembroke

Chapter 1: Becoming an Ancestry Detective: Your First Steps

Welcome to the Journey: Why Explore Your Family History?

Have you ever looked at an old photograph of a stern-faced ancestor and wondered about their life? What were their dreams? What challenges did they face? What stories are hidden behind those eyes? If so, you've already felt the tug of the past, the innate human curiosity about where we come from. Welcome to the fascinating world of genealogy, where you become the detective, piecing together the clues that tell the story of *you*.

Exploring your family history is more than just collecting names and dates. It's a journey of discovery that can connect you to the past generations, help you understand your identity, and provide a deeper appreciation for the lives and experiences of those who came before you. It's about understanding the context of your existence, the historical tides that carried your ancestors to certain shores, the economic realities that shaped their decisions, and the cultural landscapes that defined their daily lives. It's about seeing patterns, resilience, migration, adaptation, and sometimes, surprising twists of fate that led to your being here, now.

Charles Pembroke

Think of it as assembling a vast, intricate puzzle where the pieces are scattered across time and place. Each document, each photograph, and whispered family story is a potential clue waiting for you, the ancestry detective, to find it, analyze it, and fit it into the bigger picture. It's a process that requires patience, curiosity, and a willingness to follow the trail wherever it leads. But the rewards are immense: a richer understanding of yourself, a connection to a broader human story, and a tangible link to the past that can be shared with future generations.

Perhaps you've always been the designated family historian, holding onto old documents and listening intently to your elders' stories. Or maybe the interest is brand new, sparked by a television show, a conversation, or a quiet moment of reflection on your place in the world. No matter the impetus, the desire to know our origins is powerful. It speaks to a fundamental human need to belong, to understand the forces that shaped not just the world, but our lineage.

This journey can be deeply personal and profoundly moving. You may uncover tales of courage in the face of adversity, stories of migration to unknown lands in search of a better life, or simply the quiet, persistent lives of ordinary people navigating their times. You might discover unexpected connections to historical events or places you thought had no bearing on your life. You may find joyful and challenging surprises as you peel back the layers of time. But every discovery, every piece of the puzzle, adds to the rich tapestry of your family's unique history.

The Ancestry Detective

Beyond the personal rewards, there's a growing appreciation for the value of family history in a broader context. In an increasingly globalized and rapidly changing world, understanding our roots can provide a sense of stability and continuity. It can foster empathy and understanding for the experiences of different generations and cultures. It can even contribute to historical research by bringing to light the stories of ordinary people whose lives might otherwise be overlooked in the grand narratives of history.

This book is your guide to becoming an effective ancestry detective. We will equip you with the knowledge, tools, and techniques to embark on this exciting journey. We will cover the fundamental principles of genealogical research, introduce you to the key resources available, and help you develop the skills to find, interpret, and organize the clues you uncover. We'll also address some of the challenges you might encounter and how to overcome them. So, take a deep breath, sharpen your pencil (or charge your tablet!), and prepare to enter the past. Your ancestors are waiting to meet you.

Setting Your Goals: What Do You Hope to Discover?

Before you dive headfirst into searching databases and digging through old boxes, it's helpful to pause and consider what you hope to achieve. Even if they evolve, setting clear goals will help focus your research and prevent you from becoming overwhelmed by the sheer volume of potential information.

Charles Pembroke

Are you hoping to trace a specific family line back as far as possible? Are you curious about the origin of your surname? Do you want to find out if a family legend is true? Are you trying to connect with living relatives you've never met? Do you want to understand the historical context of your ancestors' lives?

Your goals can be as broad or as specific as you like. Perhaps your initial goal is to fill in the basic details (birth, marriage, death dates and places) for your grandparents and great-grandparents. This is a fantastic and manageable starting point. As you gain experience and confidence, your goals might expand to include tracing all the descendants of a particular ancestor, researching the history of a family property, or even writing a comprehensive family history narrative.

Thinking about your goals early on will help you prioritize your research efforts. Suppose you're particularly interested in a family legend about a distant relative who was a pirate (a common and often apocryphal tale!). In that case, you might focus your initial research on that individual and the period in question. If you're trying to connect with living relatives, your focus might be identifying and locating cousins and other extended family members.

It's also important to be realistic about what you can achieve, especially when starting. Genealogical research can be time-consuming, and some records can be challenging to access or interpret. You may encounter "brick walls" – points in your study where you can't find the next piece of information. Setting smaller, achievable goals can help maintain your motivation and give you a sense of accomplishment. Celebrate those small victories – finding a marriage record, confirming a birth date, or connecting with a distant cousin.

Your goals may also be influenced by the information you already have. If you have a lot of details about one side of your family but very little about another, your initial goal might be to balance that out. If you have access to specific family documents, your goals might center around verifying and expanding upon the information in those records.

Don't be afraid to revise your goals as you progress. Genealogical research is often a dynamic process, and discoveries can open up new avenues of inquiry. You might start out wanting to trace one surname and end up fascinated by the migration patterns of all your ancestral lines. The key is to have some direction to guide your initial steps and to remain open to the unexpected turns the journey might take.

Jot down your initial goals. Please keep them in your research notebook or a digital document. Refer to them periodically to ensure your research remains focused and track your progress. Knowing what you hope to find will be a powerful motivator as you delve deeper into your family's past.

The Detective's Mindset: Principles of Genealogical Research

Successful ancestry detectives operate with a specific mindset, guided by core principles that ensure the accuracy and reliability of their findings. These principles are the bedrock of sound genealogical research and will help you build a solid and trustworthy family history.

1. **Start with the Known and Work Backwards:** This is the golden rule of genealogy. Begin with yourself and move backward in time, generation by generation. Do not jump to conclusions or try to connect yourself to a famous historical figure based on a hunch or a shared surname. Work from documented facts about yourself, then your parents, grandparents, etc. Each generation you successfully document provides a solid foundation for researching the previous one.
2. **Cite Your Sources:** For every piece of information you find – a birth date, a name, a place of residence, a relationship – record *where* you found it. This includes the type of record (e.g., 1940 US Federal Census), the location of the record (e.g., Ancestry.com, National Archives), and any specific identifying information (e.g., roll number, page number, household number). Proper source citation is crucial for several reasons:
3. **Verification:** It allows you (and others) to go back and verify the information.
4. **Evaluation:** It helps you assess the reliability of the information based on the source.
5. **Avoiding Duplication:** It prevents you from wasting time searching for the same information again.
6. **Transparency:** It allows you to share your research with others in a clear and credible way. You don't need to be a professional historian to

cite sources effectively. A simple, consistent method is sufficient when you're starting. We'll discuss this further in Chapter 3.

7. **Seek Original Records (Primary Sources):** Whenever possible, find the original document that recorded an event (like a birth certificate created at the time of birth). These are considered primary sources and are generally the most reliable. Secondary sources (like published family histories or online family trees created by others) can provide valuable clues, but their information should always be verified with primary sources.

8. **Analyze Information Critically:** Don't accept everything you find at face value, especially information found in online family trees created by others. Look for inconsistencies between different records. Does a census record contradict a death certificate? Does a family story align with documented facts? Be a skeptical but open-minded detective, constantly evaluating the information you find.

9. **Understand Direct vs. Indirect Evidence:** Direct evidence explicitly states a fact (e.g., a marriage certificate listing the bride and groom). Indirect or circumstantial evidence implies a point but doesn't state it directly (e.g., a person appearing in consecutive census records in the exact location suggests they lived there continuously, but doesn't definitively prove it). Both types of evidence are valuable, but

understanding the distinction helps you build a stronger case for your conclusions.
10. **Prove Each Generational Link:** Do not assume a relationship exists because two people with the same surname lived in the same area. You need to find evidence that explicitly states or strongly implies the familial connection between generations (e.g., a birth certificate listing parents, a will naming children).
11. **Apply the FAN Principle (Family, Associates, Neighbors):** Sometimes, you can't find direct records for your ancestor. In these cases, researching the people they interacted with – their family, friends, associates (business partners, church members), and neighbors – can provide crucial clues and indirect evidence about your ancestor. People often moved and interacted within kinship and community networks.
12. **Be Persistent:** Genealogical research can be challenging, and you will encounter roadblocks. Don't get discouraged! Take a break, revisit your goals, and try new search strategies or sources. Many genealogical puzzles are solved through persistence and creative problem-solving.
13. **Share Your Findings (and Sources):** Genealogy is collaborative. Sharing your research with other family members and the wider genealogical community can lead to discoveries and connections. When you share, always include your sources so others can evaluate and build upon your work.

Embracing these principles from the beginning will set you on the path to becoming a skilled and successful ancestry detective, ensuring that the family history you uncover is as accurate and complete as possible.

Essential Tools of the Trade: Notebooks, Software, and Online Accounts

Like any good detective, you'll need tools to help you on your ancestry journey. Fortunately, the basic tools are relatively simple and can be adapted to your preferences and budget.

- **Notebook and Pens:** A physical notebook is invaluable even in the digital age. Use it to jot down ideas, sketch quick family trees, record information from phone calls with relatives, or make notes while browsing records in an archive or library. A dedicated notebook keeps your initial thoughts and findings in one place.
- **Research Log:** A research log, whether a physical notebook, a spreadsheet, or a dedicated genealogy software feature, is essential (as we'll discuss in the next section).
- **Pedigree Charts and Family Group Sheets:** These are fundamental genealogical forms. A pedigree chart in a tree format shows your direct ancestors (parents, grandparents, great-grandparents, etc.). A family group sheet details information about a single nuclear family

(parents and their children). You can find free printable versions online or use forms provided by genealogy software.

- **Computer or Tablet:** While not strictly essential for the first steps (interviewing relatives), a computer or tablet will quickly become indispensable for accessing online databases, using genealogy software, and organizing digital records.
- **Internet Access:** Most modern genealogical research involves online resources, so reliable internet access is crucial.
- **Genealogy Software (Optional but Recommended):** As your research grows, dedicated genealogy software can help you organize your family tree, link sources to individuals, and generate reports and charts. Many options are available, ranging from free basic programs to paid software with advanced features. Some popular choices include Family Tree Maker, Legacy Family Tree, RootsMagic, and online platforms like Ancestry and FamilySearch, which also have tree-building capabilities. Try a free trial or basic version to see what works best.
- **Online Genealogy Account(s):** Accessing major online databases will likely require subscriptions to platforms like Ancestry, Findmypast, or MyHeritage. Many offer free trials or basic free accounts that allow you to start building a tree. FamilySearch is a large, free platform run by the Church of Jesus Christ of

Latter-day Saints and is an excellent resource for beginners and experienced researchers alike.

- **Scanner or Smartphone Scanner App:** As you collect physical documents and photos, you'll want to digitize them to preserve them and make them easily accessible for research and sharing. A flatbed scanner or a good smartphone scanning app will be handy.
- **Cloud Storage Account:** Storing digital copies of your records and your genealogy files in a cloud service (like Google Drive, Dropbox, or OneDrive) provides a secure backup and allows you to access your research from multiple devices.

Don't feel you need to acquire all these tools simultaneously. Start with the basics – a notebook, pedigree charts, and access to the internet. As your research progresses and your needs evolve, you can invest in additional tools like genealogy software or paid online subscriptions. The most important tool is your curiosity and dedication.

Beginning Your Research Log: Why Documentation is Crucial

Imagine this scenario: you spend hours searching an online database, finding several promising records for an ancestor. You jot down a few notes on a scrap of paper, feeling confident you can easily find them again. You want to revisit those records a few weeks later, but you can't remember which database you used, what search terms you entered, or where you saved those scattered notes. Frustrating, right?

This is where a research log becomes your best friend. A research log is a systematic record of every search you conduct, regardless of whether you find what you're looking for. It's a detective's case file, detailing every lead followed and every avenue explored.

Why is a research log crucial for an ancestry detective, especially a beginner?

1. **Avoids Duplication:** It prevents you from wasting precious time and potentially money (on subscriptions or record requests) by repeating searches you've already performed.

2. **Tracks Your Progress:** It provides a clear overview of what you've done and what areas of your family tree you've focused on.

3. **Identifies Brick Walls:** When you hit a point where you can't find information, your research log will show you all the sources you've already checked, helping you identify what hasn't been explored yet.

4. **Helps You Plan Next Steps:** By seeing what you've already searched, you can make informed decisions about where to look.

5. **Documents Negative Results:** Recording searches that *didn't* yield results is just as important as recording successful ones. It tells you that a particular source does not contain the information you seek.

6. **Supports Source Citation:** Your research log naturally feeds into your source citations, making it easier to document where you found your information accurately.

7. **Provides a Roadmap for Others:** If you ever share your research or need help from another genealogist, your research log provides them with a clear understanding of the work you've already done.

What should you include in your research log? For each search, record:

- **Date of Search:** When you performed the search.
- **Ancestor(s) Being Researched:** The individual(s) you were looking for.
- **Record Type:** The type of record you were searching (e.g., census, marriage records, passenger lists).
- **Location of Record:** The database, archive, library, or website you used.
- **Search Terms Used:** The names, dates, and places you entered into the search engine or index.
- **Result of Search:** Did you find relevant information? If yes, briefly describe what you found. If no, state that you didn't find anything.
- **Source Citation Information:** Enough detail to allow you to create a full source citation later (e.g., volume number, page number, file name).

- **Notes/Analysis:** Any thoughts or observations about the search or the records found.

Your research log can be as simple as a dedicated notebook with columns for each piece of information, a spreadsheet created in Excel or Google Sheets, or a feature within your chosen genealogy software. The key is to consistently and diligently record your searches from the beginning. It might seem tedious initially, but it will save you countless hours of frustration in the long run and is a hallmark of a disciplined ancestry detective.

Understanding Privacy and Ethics: Researching Living Relatives

As you embark on your genealogical journey, you will likely gather information about deceased and living individuals. When researching living relatives, it is crucial to proceed with sensitivity, respect for privacy, and a strong ethical compass.

Unlike historical records, which are generally publicly accessible after a specific period, privacy laws and ethical considerations protect information about living individuals. Sharing personal details about living people without their consent is a breach of trust and potentially illegal.

Here are some key points to consider:
- **Obtain Consent Before Sharing Information:** Before sharing any information you

gather about living relatives (including names, dates, places of birth, marriage, residence, or any personal details) with others outside of your immediate family, always ask for their explicit permission. This applies to sharing information in online family trees, published materials, or even casual conversations with distant relatives you find.

- **Be Mindful of Online Family Trees:** Many online genealogy platforms allow users to create and share family trees. When adding living individuals to an online tree, ensure the platform's privacy settings are configured to hide information about living people from public view. Reputable platforms have features to protect the privacy of living individuals.
- **Respect Requests for Privacy:** If a relative expresses discomfort with sharing certain information or prefers not to be included in your research or online tree, respect their wishes without question or pressure. Your relationship with living family members is far more important than adding one more name to your tree.
- **Be Sensitive When Asking Questions:** When interviewing living relatives, remember that some topics may be sensitive or bring up painful memories. Approach questions empathetically and be prepared to change the subject if someone seems uncomfortable. Avoid prying into off-limits areas.

- **Handle Adoption and Sensitive Family Situations with Care:** Genealogical research can sometimes uncover adoptions, unexpected parentage, or other sensitive family situations. Approach these discoveries with immense sensitivity and discretion. If you find information that a living relative may not be aware of, consider the potential impact before sharing it and think carefully about who, if anyone, you should inform and how. In many cases, it may be best to handle such information with extreme privacy or seek guidance from experienced genealogists or counsellors.
- **Understand Legal and Ethical Guidelines:** Be aware of privacy laws in the locations where your relatives live, particularly when dealing with vital records of recently deceased individuals. Genealogical organizations often have ethical guidelines that provide valuable frameworks for responsible research.

Building trust with your relatives is essential for gathering information and fostering connections. Demonstrating respect for their privacy and being ethical in your research practices can build stronger relationships and ensure that your pursuit of family history is a positive experience for everyone involved. Remember, your role as an ancestry detective extends beyond uncovering the past to responsibly handling the present.

Avoiding Common Pitfalls: Surname Myths, Brick Walls, and Online Rumors

The path of the ancestry detective is not always smooth. Common pitfalls can lead you down the wrong path, cause frustration, and even result in inaccurate conclusions. Knowing these traps from the beginning will help you navigate them more effectively.

1. **Surname Myths and Legends:** Many families have cherished stories about the origin of their surname, its meaning, or a famous (or infamous) ancestor who first bore the name. While these stories can be fascinating, they are often inaccurate or embellished over generations. Do not assume a connection to a particular historical figure or event based solely on a shared surname. Surnames can change over time, multiple unrelated families can have the same surname, and the meaning or origin of a name can be complex. Your research must be based on documented proof of lineage, not just a shared name.

2. **Hitting a "Brick Wall":** A brick wall is a point in your research where you cannot find any further information about a specific ancestor or family line. This is a common and often frustrating experience in genealogy. Brick walls can occur for various reasons: records may have been lost or destroyed, ancestors may have lived in areas with poor record-keeping, or they may have intentionally obscured their past. Don't

despair when you hit a brick wall. This is often where the real detective work begins! Later chapters will explore strategies for overcoming brick walls, including researching associates and neighbors, exploring alternative record types, and utilizing DNA evidence.

3. **Blindly Trusting Online Trees:** Online genealogy platforms are wonderful resources, and the user-submitted family trees can provide valuable clues. However, it is absolutely crucial to treat information in online trees as *hints* or *leads*, not as proven facts. The accuracy of these trees varies wildly depending on the research skills and diligence of the person who created them. Information is often copied from other trees without verification, perpetuating errors. Always verify any information you find in an online tree with original sources. Look for trees that include source citations – this is a good sign, but still verify the sources yourself if possible.

4. **Making Assumptions:** Avoid making assumptions based on limited information. For example, don't assume that two people with the same surname living in the same town are related without evidence. Don't assume that an ancestor's birthplace listed in one record is definitively correct, as people sometimes provided inconsistent information. Base your conclusions on documented evidence and be open to revising your theories as you find new information.

5. **Ignoring Historical Context:** To truly understand your ancestors' lives, you need to understand the historical context in which they lived. What were the significant events in their time and place, as well as social norms, economic conditions, and migration patterns? Ignoring this context can lead to misinterpretations of records and a less complete understanding of their experiences. For example, understanding the history of immigration patterns can help you interpret passenger lists and naturalization records.

6. **Getting Overwhelmed:** The sheer volume of potential records and information can be daunting for a beginner. To avoid feeling overwhelmed, start small, set achievable goals, and focus on one or two family lines at a time. Organize your research systematically, and don't be afraid to take breaks when needed.

7. **Not Citing Sources from the Start:** We've already emphasized this, but it's worth repeating as a major pitfall. Failing to cite your sources from the beginning will make it incredibly difficult to verify your findings, track your research, and share your work accurately later on.

By being aware of these common pitfalls and adopting the principles of sound genealogical research, you can navigate your ancestry journey more effectively and build a family history that is both accurate and meaningful.

Getting Organized from the Start: Creating a Dedicated Workspace

Embarking on your ancestry detective work can quickly lead to a proliferation of papers, documents, notes, and digital files. To maintain your sanity and ensure efficient research, it is essential to establish a dedicated workspace and implement an organizational system from day one. Trying to organize a mountain of unsorted information retroactively is a far more challenging task.

Your dedicated workspace doesn't need to be a large, elaborate office. It could be a corner of a room, a desk, or even a designated box or file cabinet where you keep all your genealogy materials. The key is to have a central location where everything related to your research is stored.

Here's what to consider when setting up your workspace and organizational system:

- **Physical Storage:** You will accumulate physical documents, photocopies, printouts of online records, and notes. Invest in filing cabinets, binders, or sturdy boxes to store these materials. Decide on a logical filing system—perhaps by surname, family group, or location. Consistency is more important than the specific system you choose initially. Label everything clearly.
- **Digital Storage:** Your digital files include scanned documents, downloaded records, photos, genealogy software files, and research logs. Create a clear folder structure on your

computer or in a cloud storage service. A common approach is to create a main genealogy folder with subfolders for each surname or family line, and then further subfolders within those for different record types (e.g., Census, Vital Records, Photos). Use a consistent naming convention for your digital files (e.g., "Smith_John_1900Census_NewYork.pdf").

- **Research Log Location:** Decide where you will keep your research log – in your physical notebook, a spreadsheet, or within your genealogy software. Keep it easily accessible while you are researching.
- **In-Progress Area:** Designate an area for documents or tasks you are currently working on. This could be a tray on your desk or a specific digital folder. This prevents active projects from getting lost in your main filing system.
- **Supplies:** Keep essential supplies handy, such as pens, pencils, highlighters (for marking key information on copies), sticky notes, a stapler, and paper clips.
- **Technology Setup:** Ensure your computer or tablet is set up comfortably with reliable internet access. If you have a scanner, have it easily accessible.
- **Comfort and Lighting:** Choose a comfortable workspace with adequate lighting. You'll be spending a reasonable amount of time here!
- **Regular Maintenance:** Schedule regular time to tidy your workspace and file new

documents and digital files. Letting things pile up will quickly lead to disorganization.

Think of your organizational system as the backbone of your research. A well-organized system will save you time, reduce frustration, and ensure that you can easily find the information you need when you need it. Starting small and building your system as your research grows is acceptable, but the crucial part is organizing from the first document you acquire.

Building Your Foundation: The Initial Pedigree Chart and Family Group Sheets

Before you delve into extensive record searching, you must lay a solid foundation by documenting what you already know. The primary tools for this initial step are the pedigree chart and the family group sheet. These standardized forms provide a clear and organized way to record your known ancestors and their immediate families.

- **The Pedigree Chart:** This chart visually displays your direct ancestral lines. It starts with you (Generation 1), then lists your parents (Generation 2), your grandparents (Generation 3), your great-grandparents (Generation 4), and so on. Each generation doubles the number of ancestors on the chart (2 parents, 4 grandparents, 8 great-grandparents, 16 great-great-grandparents, etc.).

- **How to Fill It Out:** Enter your name and vital information (birth date and place, marriage date and place, death date and place if applicable) in the designated spot (usually the far left). Then, move to Generation 2 and enter the information for your father and mother, linking them to you. Continue backward, adding the information for your paternal grandparents, maternal grandparents, and so on.
- **What to Include:** For each individual, include their full name (including maiden names for women), and as much vital information as you know (birth, marriage, and death dates and places). There are also spaces for their spouse's name and the location where information about that spouse can be found (often a family group sheet number).
- **Benefits:** The pedigree chart provides a clear visual overview of your direct ancestry and quickly shows you where the gaps in your knowledge exist (blank spaces are your research opportunities!).

- **The Family Group Sheet:** This sheet focuses on a single nuclear family: a set of parents and all of their children.

- **How to Fill It Out:** Create a separate family group sheet for each couple in your direct ancestral lines (and eventually for the families of siblings and other relatives you research). At the top, enter the names and vital information for the

husband and wife. Below that, list all of their children, including their essential information and, if known, the names of their spouses.
- **What to Include:** For the parents and each child, include full name, birth date and place, marriage date and place, and death date and place. There are also spaces to record your information sources for each fact.
- **Benefits:** The family group sheet allows you to record detailed information about each family unit, including all siblings, which is crucial for applying the FAN principle and understanding the broader family context. It also provides a clear place to record sources for specific facts about each individual within that family group.

You can download free printable pedigree charts and family group sheets from numerous genealogical websites (FamilySearch and Ancestry often provide them). Alternatively, most genealogy software programs will generate these forms automatically as you enter information.

Start by filling out these charts with everything you already know from personal knowledge, family documents (birth certificates, marriage licenses, family Bibles, letters), and information gathered from interviewing relatives (as discussed in Chapter 2). Don't worry if there are many blank spaces – those are the starting points for your research! You will update and expand these foundational charts as you find new information. They are living documents that will grow along with your research. Building this initial foundation will provide a clear roadmap for your ancestry detective work.

Looking Ahead: What This Book Will Help You Achieve

You've taken the first crucial steps: you've felt the call to explore your family history, you've started thinking about your goals, you're adopting the mindset of a detective, and you're beginning to gather your initial information and tools. This is just the beginning of an enriching journey.

"The Ancestry Detective" is designed to be your comprehensive guide as you navigate the exciting world of genealogical research. In the coming chapters, we will delve deeper into the techniques and resources that will empower you to uncover your ancestors' stories.

We will explore the vast landscape of genealogical records, from the fundamental vital records (births, marriages, and deaths) and the illuminating census records that provide snapshots of families in time, to the rich details found in immigration papers, military service files, land ownership documents, and probate records. You will learn how to locate these records in traditional archives and the ever-expanding online databases and critically interpret their information.

We will also explore the revolutionary impact of DNA testing on genealogy, understanding how genetic evidence can complement your document-based research, break down stubborn brick walls, and connect you with previously unknown relatives.

Beyond finding names and dates, this book will guide you in piecing together the narratives of your ancestors' lives. You will learn how to place their experiences within their historical context and understand the social, economic, and political forces that shaped their world.

Finally, we will explore ways to organize, preserve, and share your discoveries, transforming your research into a lasting legacy that can be passed down to future generations. Whether you aspire to write a family history book, create an engaging online tree, or share stories and documents with your relatives, we will provide the tools and inspiration to bring your family's history to life.

Becoming an ancestry detective is a journey of discovery that can enrich your understanding of yourself and your place in the world. It requires patience, curiosity, and a willingness to learn. But with the right tools, techniques, and a detective's mindset, you are well-equipped to embark on this exciting adventure into the past. Your ancestors' stories are waiting to be uncovered, and you are the perfect person to find them. Let's begin.

Chapter 2: Starting with the Known: Interviewing Your Relatives

You've embraced the call to become an ancestry detective, have a sense of your goals, and understand the foundational principles of good research. Now, it's time to begin the active investigation, and the absolute best place to start is with the people who hold the most readily available clues: your living relatives. Think of them as your initial informants, possessing a wealth of knowledge, memories, and perhaps even tangible evidence like old photographs or documents, all waiting to be discovered.

The Richest Source: Why Living Relatives Are Invaluable

In the exciting world of genealogy, where online databases and historical archives often feel like the main event, it might seem counterintuitive to begin your quest by simply having conversations. However, experienced genealogists will tell you that some of the most valuable information and inspiring stories come directly from those who lived them or heard about them firsthand from those who did. Your living relatives are unique and irreplaceable resources, and engaging with them should be your first priority as an ancestry detective.

Why are living relatives such a rich source of information?

1. **Firsthand Knowledge:** They possess personal memories of events, people, and places that may not be recorded elsewhere. Their recollections of birthdays, holidays, family gatherings, personality quirks, and everyday life can bring your ancestors to life in a way that dry facts and dates cannot.
2. **Connecting Generations:** Older relatives, in particular, can bridge gaps between generations. They may have known grandparents, great-grandparents, or even more distant relatives, carrying forward stories and details passed down orally.
3. **Identifying Key Individuals:** Your relatives can provide names of parents, grandparents, siblings, aunts, uncles, and cousins, immediately expanding your known family tree. They can also help you identify which branches of the family are most interesting to you or where potential "low-hanging fruit" for research might exist.
4. **Locating Documents and Artifacts:** Family members are often the custodians of precious family heirlooms, photographs, letters, diaries, certificates, military records, and other documents. These tangible items are primary sources that can verify information, provide new clues, and add depth to your understanding. A casual mention of "that old family Bible" or "a

box of Grandma's letters" can open up entirely new avenues of research.

5. Understanding Family Relationships and Dynamics: Relatives can illuminate the complex web of family relationships, including marriages, divorces, adoptions, and less formal connections. They can describe family dynamics, traditions, and even long-held feuds or secrets, providing context for later discoveries in official records.

6. Pronunciation and Spelling Clues: Family members can tell you how names were pronounced, which can be incredibly helpful when dealing with variations in spelling found in historical records. They might also know about nicknames or alternative names used by ancestors.

7. Geographical Information: Relatives often know where family members lived, worked, attended school, or attended church. This geographical information is vital for locating records, as many historical documents are organized by location.

8. Setting the Stage for Further Research: The information you gather from interviews provides the essential framework for your documentary research. It gives you names, dates (even if approximate), places, and relationships to search for in online databases and archives. Without this initial step, you might be searching blindly.

9. **Building Rapport and Engaging the Family:** Interviewing relatives is not just about extracting information; it's also about connecting with your family and sharing your interest in your shared history. This can spark interest in others and potentially lead to collaborative research efforts. It's a chance to strengthen family bonds and create a shared sense of heritage.

10. **Capturing Fleeting Memories:** Memories fade over time. The sooner you speak with your older relatives, the more detailed and accurate their recollections will likely be. The information they hold is a precious, finite resource that should be captured before it is lost.

Think of each interview as a unique opportunity to gather puzzle pieces that only your relative possesses. These conversations can fill in the gaps between the official records, providing the human stories and personal details that make your family history truly come alive. Do not underestimate the power of these personal connections – they are the heart and soul of your ancestry detective work.

Planning Your Interviews: Identifying Key Relatives and Preparing Questions

Approaching your relatives for information requires thoughtful planning. Simply showing up with a blank notebook and asking, "So, tell me about the family," is unlikely to yield the best results. A little preparation can make your interviews more productive, enjoyable, and respectful of your relatives' time and memories.

1. **Identify Your Key Relatives:** Who should you interview first? Start with the oldest living relatives in each branch of your family that you are researching. They are most likely to know earlier generations. However, don't overlook younger relatives; they may have different memories, perspectives, or even be the custodians of different family artifacts. Consider siblings, cousins, aunts, and uncles. Think broadly about who might have valuable information.
2. **Prioritize Your Interviews:** If you have many relatives, you might need to prioritize based on age, health, location, and willingness to participate. Start with those whose health is declining or who are most enthusiastic about sharing their memories.
3. **Contact Your Relatives and Explain Your Project:** Reach out to your relatives and explain that you are starting to research your family history and would love to talk with them. Briefly explain what you hope to achieve and why their contribution is important. Be clear about the time commitment you are requesting. Asking in advance allows them to feel prepared and willing to share.
4. **Be Flexible and Accommodating:** Your relatives are doing you a favor by sharing their time and memories. Be flexible with scheduling and be

willing to meet at a time and location that is convenient for them. Offer to travel to them if possible.
5. **Prepare Your Questions in Advance:** This is crucial for guiding the conversation and ensuring you cover the areas you are most interested in. While you want the conversation to flow naturally, having a list of prepared questions will keep you on track and prompt memories. Organize your questions by topic or by individual.
6. **Tailor Your Questions:** Consider what each specific relative might know. An older aunt might have vivid memories of your grandmother's childhood, while a cousin might have information about a more recent generation or a different family branch. Tailor your questions to their likely knowledge and experiences.
7. **Start with Open-Ended Questions:** Avoid questions that can be answered with a simple "yes" or "no." Instead, ask questions that encourage your relative to elaborate and tell stories. Examples:
    - "What do you remember about your grandparents?"
    - "Can you tell me about your childhood?"
    - "What was life like in [place where they lived] when you were growing up?"
    - "How did your parents meet?"
    - "What were some of your family's traditions?"
    - "Do you remember any stories about [specific ancestor]?"

8. **Ask About Specific Facts:** While stories are invaluable, also ask about specific details like full names (including maiden names), birth dates and places, marriage dates and places, death dates and places, occupations, schools attended, places of residence, and names of siblings and their spouses. Be prepared for approximations; even an approximate year or location is a valuable clue.
9. **Ask About Documents and Photos:** Ask if they have any old photographs, letters, diaries, certificates, family Bibles, military papers, or other documents. Express your interest in seeing and potentially making copies of these items.
10. **Include Questions About Family Lore and Legends:** Ask about any family stories or legends that have been passed down. While these may not be entirely accurate, they often contain kernels of truth and can point you towards areas for further research.
11. **Organize Your Questions Logically:** Group related questions together to help the conversation flow smoothly. You might start with general questions about their earliest memories and then move to specific individuals or periods.
12. **Practice Active Listening:** Prepare to listen more than you talk. Your role is to facilitate sharing memories, not dominate the conversation.

Preparing for your interviews demonstrates respect for your relatives' time and helps you get the most out of these valuable conversations. It sets the stage for a productive and enjoyable information-gathering session.

Conducting the Interview: Techniques for Eliciting Information and Building Rapport

1. The interview itself is where the magic happens. It's a chance to connect with your relatives on a deeper level and unlock the treasures of their memories. Approach the interview with enthusiasm, patience, and a genuine interest in what your relative shares.
2. **Choose a Comfortable Setting:** Conduct the interview in a quiet, comfortable environment where your relative feels relaxed and can talk without interruptions. Their home is often the best place, as they may have documents or photos readily available.
3. **Start with Casual Conversation:** Chat about everyday things to help your relative feel at ease. Don't jump straight into your list of questions. Build rapport and create a relaxed atmosphere.
4. **Explain Your Recording Plan:** If you plan to record the interview (which is highly recommended), explain this to your relative at the beginning and get their explicit permission *before* you start recording. Please explain why you want to record (to ensure you don't miss anything and to preserve their voice and stories).
5. **Use Your Prepared Questions as a Guide, Not a Script:** Your list of questions keeps you on

track, but don't be afraid to deviate if the conversation takes an interesting turn. Follow your relative's lead and explore the tangents they introduce; unexpected and valuable information often lies just off the planned path.

6. **Practice Active Listening:** Pay close attention to what your relative is saying. Nod, make eye contact, and offer verbal cues like "Mm-hmm" or "Go on." This shows you are engaged and encourages them to continue sharing.

7. **Ask Follow-Up Questions:** Don't move on to the next question on your list once your relative has finished their initial answer. Ask follow-up questions to encourage them to elaborate. "Can you tell me more about that?" "What was that like?" "Do you remember who else was there?"

8. **Be Patient with Pauses and Silences:** Memories can take time to surface. Be patient and allow for pauses and silences. Avoid interrupting or finishing their sentences. Sometimes, the most valuable memories emerge after a period of quiet reflection.

9. **Ask for Clarification:** Politely ask for clarification if something is unclear. "Could you spell that name for me?" "Could you tell me more about where that was located?"

10. **Handle Inaccuracies Gently:** Your relative's memory may not be perfect, and they may inadvertently provide information that you later find inaccurate based on records. Do not correct them or challenge their memories during the interview. Make a note and plan to verify the

information later with documentary evidence. The goal of the interview is to capture their recollections as they remember them.

11. **Be Mindful of Time:** Respect your relative's time and energy levels. If you agreed on a specific time limit, stick to it. If the interview is going well and your relative is willing to continue, ask if they would like to extend it or schedule a follow-up session.

12. **Thank Your Relative Enthusiastically:** At the end of the interview, express your sincere gratitude for their time, willingness to share their memories, and invaluable contribution to your family history project. Let them know how much their stories mean to you.

13. **Take Brief Notes During the Interview:** Even if you are recording, taking brief notes can help you remember key points, spellings of names, and things you want to follow up on later. However, don't let note-taking distract you from actively listening.

Conducting effective interviews is a skill that improves with practice. Approach each conversation with genuine curiosity and a deep appreciation for the gift of your relative's memories. These interviews will provide you with crucial genealogical information, create cherished moments, and strengthen your family connections.

Recording the Conversation: Audio, Video, and Note-Taking

Capturing your relatives' memories accurately is paramount. Relying solely on your memory during or after the interview is unreliable. Fortunately, there are several methods for recording the conversation, each with its advantages.

1. **Audio Recording:**
   - **Advantages:** Captures every word, including nuances of voice and emotion. Allows you to focus on the conversation rather than constantly taking notes. Relatively easy to do with readily available technology.
   - **Methods:**
     - **Smartphone Voice Recorder:** Most smartphones have simple-to-use built-in voice recording apps. Ensure you have enough storage space and that the phone is fully charged.
     - **Digital Voice Recorder:** Dedicated digital voice recorders often offer better audio quality and longer recording times than smartphones.
     - **Computer Software:** You can use recording software on a laptop if you are interviewing via video call or in person with a computer present.
   - **Tips for Audio Recording:**

- **Always Get Permission:** Reiterate that you are recording and get explicit consent.
- **Test Your Equipment:** Before the interview, do a test recording to ensure the microphone works and the sound quality is acceptable.
- **Minimize Background Noise:** Choose a quiet location for the interview.
- **Place the Recorder Appropriately:** Position the recorder close enough to your relative to capture their voice.
- **Announce the Start of the Recording:** State the date, location, and the name of the person being interviewed at the beginning of the recording.
- **Monitor the Recording:** Periodically check that the recording is still active.

2. **Video Recording:**
    - **Advantages:** Captures not only voice but also facial expressions, body language, and the environment. Preserves a more complete sensory experience of the interview. Great for capturing reactions when showing photos or documents.
    - **Methods:**
        - **Smartphone or Tablet Video Recorder:** Modern smartphones and tablets record high-quality video.

- **Digital Camera or Camcorder:** Dedicated video recording devices offer more advanced features and often better quality.
- **Webcam and Video Conferencing Software:** If conducting the interview remotely, use video conferencing software (like Zoom, Skype, or Google Meet), which often have recording capabilities.

○ **Tips for Video Recording:**
- **Always Get Permission:** Crucial for video recording due to the visual element.
- **Consider Lighting and Background:** Choose a well-lit location with a tidy background.
- **Position the Camera Steadily:** Use a tripod or stable surface to avoid shaky footage.
- **Frame Your Subject Well:** Ensure your relative is visible in the frame.
- **Test Your Equipment:** Check video and audio quality before starting.
- **Announce the Start:** State the interview details at the beginning of the recording.

3. **Note-Taking:**
   ○ **Advantages:** Provides a quick way to jot down key facts, names, dates, and ideas for follow-up questions during the interview. Useful

as a backup even when recording audio or video. Helps you stay engaged by actively processing the information.
- **Methods:**
  - **Physical Notebook:** Simple and requires no technology.
  - **Laptop or Tablet:** Allows for faster typing and easier organization of notes.
- **Tips for Note-Taking:**
  - **Develop a System of Abbreviations:** To quickly jot down standard terms.
  - **Focus on Key Information:** Don't try to write down every word.
  - **Note Things to Follow Up On:** Use a symbol or mark to indicate points you want to ask about later.
  - **Record Names and Spellings Carefully:** Ask for clarification if unsure.
  - **Jot Down Impressions and Observations:** Note your relative's demeanor or any interesting non-verbal cues.

Combining Methods: Many genealogists use a combination of recording methods. For example, you might audio record the entire conversation while also taking brief written notes to mark key points or spellings. If you are showing photos, you might use video recording for that portion of the interview.

Post-Interview Processing: Regardless of how you record the interview, the work doesn't end when you turn off the recorder.

- **Transcribe Recordings:** If you have audio or video recordings, transcribe them as soon as possible while the conversation is fresh in your mind. This makes the information easily searchable and reviewable. You can transcribe them yourself, use transcription software, or use transcription services.
- **Organize Your Notes and Recordings:** Store your interview notes and recordings in your dedicated genealogy workspace, linked to the relevant individuals or family groups in your research system.
- **Synthesize the Information:** Review your notes and transcriptions and begin to extract key pieces of information to add to your family tree, research log, and individual profiles.

Choosing the right recording method and processing the information diligently after the interview are vital steps in ensuring that the valuable memories shared by your relatives are accurately captured and preserved for your ancestry detective work.

Beyond the Facts: Eliciting Stories, Memories, and Family Lore

While names, dates, and places are the building blocks of genealogy, the true richness of family history lies in the stories, memories, and traditions passed down through generations. These narratives breathe life into the facts and help you understand the people behind the names. As an ancestry detective, your goal should be to uncover the "who, what, when, and where," and the "how and why."

Encouraging your relatives to share stories and memories requires moving beyond a purely factual interrogation. Create an atmosphere where they feel comfortable reminiscing and sharing personal anecdotes.

- **Ask "Tell Me About..." Questions:** Instead of asking "When was your mother born?" try "Tell me about your mother's childhood." This open-ended approach invites a narrative response.
- **Prompt Memories with Sensory Details:** Ask what things looked, sounded, smelled, tasted, or felt like. "What was your grandmother's house like?" "What were the popular songs when you were young?" "What did your family eat on holidays?"
- **Ask About Everyday Life:** Don't focus solely on significant life events. Ask about daily routines, school experiences, work life, hobbies, friendships, and community involvement. These details provide valuable insights into the texture of their lives.
- **Explore Family Traditions:** Ask about holiday customs, family recipes, rituals, and inside jokes. These traditions are often significant and reveal aspects of family identity.

- **Inquire About Challenges and Triumphs:** Life isn't always easy. Ask about the difficulties your relatives faced and how they overcame them. Ask about their proudest moments and biggest accomplishments. These stories highlight resilience and character.
- **Listen for Family Lore and Legends:** Pay attention to stories passed down through the family, even if they seem fantastical. These legends often contain a kernel of truth or reflect how the family views its history. Make a note of them to investigate further with records.
- **Ask About the "Why":** When your relative shares a factual detail, try to ask "why." "Why did your family move to that town?" "Why did your father choose that profession?" Understanding the motivations behind decisions adds depth to the story.
- **Be Patient and Allow for Reflection:** Stories don't always unfold in a linear fashion. Allow yourself relative time to think and recall memories. Sometimes, one memory will trigger another, leading to unexpected insights.
- **Show Genuine Interest:** Your genuine enthusiasm for their stories will encourage your relatives to share more openly. Let them know that their memories are important and valued.
- **Don't Interrupt a Good Story:** While it's important to guide the conversation, if your relative is engrossed in telling a story, listen intently and save your questions for when they

are finished.

Capturing these stories is vital to building a rich and meaningful family history. These details will resonate with future generations and help them feel connected to the individuals on your family tree. Think of yourself as a collector of facts and a curator of family narratives.

The Power of Show and Tell: Asking About Photos, Documents, and Artifacts

Beyond their verbal recollections, your relatives may hold tangible links to the past through photographs, documents, and family artifacts. These items are often packed with clues and can trigger memories that words alone might not unlock. Incorporating a "show and tell" element into your interviews can be incredibly fruitful.

1. **Ask About Existing Items in Advance:** When you contact your relatives to schedule the interview, ask if they have any old family photos, letters, documents, or other items they would be willing to share with you during your visit. This gives them time to gather things.
2. **Go Through Photos Together:** Looking at old photographs with your relatives is a fantastic way to elicit memories. Ask them to identify the people in the photos, where and when the photos were taken, and the stories behind the images. Use your phone or a scanner to take pictures

or make copies of the photos (with permission).

3. **Examine Documents Together:** Ask about any old family documents they have, such as birth certificates, marriage licenses, passports, letters, diaries, military papers, or property deeds. Even documents that seem mundane can contain valuable genealogical information or trigger memories. Ask about the context of the document – why was it kept? Who did it belong to? Make copies of relevant documents.
4. **Explore Family Artifacts:** Objects like furniture, jewelry, tools, or handmade items can also hold stories. Ask about the history of these items – who owned them, where did they come from, do they have any special significance?
5. **Be Prepared to Digitize on Site:** If your relatives are willing, have a portable scanner or a good smartphone scanning app ready to digitize photos and documents on the spot. This ensures you get copies and your relatives don't have to part with their treasures.
6. **Document Each Item:** As you look at each photo, document, or artifact, note who is in it, what it is, when and where it was from (if known), and any stories your relative shares about it. This

documentation is crucial for identifying and cataloging these items later.

7. **Ask About Items They Don't Have:** Your relatives might mention items other family members possess. This can provide leads for future interviews.
8. **Respect the Sentimental Value:** Understand that these items may have deep sentimental value to your relatives. Handle them with care and express your appreciation for being allowed to see them. Please do not ask to keep original items unless they are explicitly offered.
9. **Use Items as Conversation Starters:** If the conversation is slow, introducing a photo or document can often spark memories and get the conversation flowing again.
10. **Return Items Promptly:** If you borrow any physical items for scanning or further examination, return them promptly and thank your relative again.

The tangible evidence held by your relatives is a goldmine for the ancestry detective. These items provide factual clues and powerful memory triggers, unlocking stories and details that might otherwise remain hidden. Make "show and tell" a key part of your interview strategy.

Interviewing Different Generations: Tailoring Your Approach

When interviewing relatives, you'll likely speak with individuals from different generations, each with unique perspectives, memories, and communication styles. Tailoring your approach to the age and experiences of your relative can make your interviews more effective and rewarding.

1. **Older Generations (Parents, Grandparents, Great-Grandparents):**
   - **Focus:** These relatives are invaluable for information about earlier generations and historical context. They are the keepers of older memories and family lore.
   - **Approach:** Be patient, listen attentively, and allow plenty of time for them to share their memories. They may have a wealth of information, but it might not come out strictly linearly. Be prepared for tangents and be respectful of their energy levels and health. Ask open-ended questions that encourage storytelling. Be particularly interested in the memories of their parents and grandparents.
   - **Tips:** Record the conversation to capture every detail. Bring old photos or documents to help jog their memories. Be mindful of potential hearing or memory challenges and adapt your communication style accordingly.

2. **Middle Generations (Aunts, Uncles, Older Cousins):**

- **Focus:** These relatives can provide details about their lives, parents, and siblings. They may have a different perspective on family events than older generations. They might also be more familiar with using technology and have digital photos or documents.
- **Approach:** Engage them in a more conversational style. They may be busy with work and family, so respect their time. Ask about their childhood, their parents, and their experiences growing up. They can often fill in details about the lives of the generation before them.
- **Tips:** Be prepared to interview them in person, over the phone, or via video call. They may be more comfortable with digital sharing of information.

3. **Younger Generations (Siblings, Younger Cousins, Children):**

- **Focus:** While they may not have memories of distant ancestors, younger relatives are valuable for documenting recent family history and ensuring the continuation of your research. They can provide information about their lives, parents, and recent family events. They are also often tech-savvy and can help with digitizing or organizing information.
- **Approach:** Engage them in a relevant way to their interests. Ask about their experiences, perspectives on family, and what aspects of family history are important. Involve them in the research process; they may enjoy learning about their ancestors and contributing to the project.

- **Tips:** Use social media or messaging apps to connect and share information. Please encourage them to record their memories and experiences for future generations.

4. **Relatives by Marriage or Adoption:**
   - **Focus:** These relatives bring unique perspectives and information about their family lines, which merge with yours. They may have documents, photos, or stories about the side of the family that married into yours.
   - **Approach:** Be welcoming and inclusive. Show genuine interest in their family history as well. The FAN principle applies here – their family members are your ancestors' associates and can hold valuable clues.

5. **Handling Group Interviews:** While one-on-one interviews are often best for in-depth conversations, you may have the opportunity to interview multiple relatives at once (e.g., siblings).
   - **Advantages:** Can spark shared memories and correct inaccuracies through discussion.
   - **Challenges:** It can be harder to control the conversation; some individuals may dominate or be reluctant to speak in a group setting.
   - **Tips:** Have a clear plan, but be flexible. Encourage everyone to participate. Be prepared for lively discussions!

Tailoring your questions and approach to the relative you are interviewing will help you build rapport and maximize the information you gather. Each generation holds a unique piece of the family history puzzle.

Handling Difficult or Sensitive Topics: Navigating Family Secrets and Trauma

You may encounter difficult or sensitive topics as you delve into your family history. These can include family secrets, strained relationships, divorce, adoption, illness, mental health struggles, criminal activity, or experiences of trauma such as war or migration under duress. Navigating these areas requires immense sensitivity, empathy, and a commitment to ethical research.

1. **Be Prepared for Unexpected Discoveries:** Your relatives may share information that surprises, upsets, or shocks you. Family histories are rarely perfect, and people have lived through challenging times. Be prepared to hear about your family's past, less glamorous or even painful aspects.

2. **Listen Without Judgment:** If a relative shares something difficult, listen with empathy and without judgment. Remember that you are hearing their personal experience or a story passed down to them. Your role is to listen, document, and not judge past actions or decisions.

3. **Respect Boundaries:** If a relative is reluctant to talk about a topic or becomes visibly distressed, do not push them. Respect their

boundaries and move on to a different subject. Let them know they do not have to share anything they are uncomfortable with.

4. **Be Mindful of Emotional Impact:** Discussing the past, especially traumatic events, can be emotionally taxing for your relatives. Be prepared for them to become emotional, and offer support and understanding. Have tissues available if needed.

5. **Handle Family Secrets with Extreme Care:** If you uncover what appears to be a family secret (e.g., an adoption that was not discussed, a previously unknown child), think very carefully before sharing this information, especially with living relatives who may be directly impacted. Consider the potential consequences and whether revealing the information would cause more harm than good. Sometimes, it may be best to keep such discoveries private or seek advice from experienced professionals.

6. **Focus on the Historical Context:** When discussing difficult historical events (like slavery, war, or persecution), try to understand the context in which your ancestors lived. This doesn't excuse complex actions, but it can help understand the circumstances they faced.

7. **Be Prepared for Different Perspectives:** Different family members may have different memories or interpretations of the same events, particularly if there was conflict or disagreement within the family. Listen to all perspectives without taking sides.

8. **Document Carefully but Discretely:** If you gather information about sensitive topics, document it accurately in your research log and notes, but be mindful of where and how you store this information, especially if others might have access to your research.

9. **Consider the Impact of Sharing:** Before sharing information about sensitive topics, particularly in a public forum like an online tree or a published history, consider the potential impact on living relatives. Obtain consent before sharing potentially sensitive details about living or recently deceased individuals.

10. **Seek Support if Needed:** Researching challenging family histories can sometimes be emotionally difficult. If you are struggling with what you uncover, talk to a trusted friend or family member, or consider seeking professional support.

Navigating complex and sensitive topics is perhaps the most challenging aspect of family history research. It requires detective skills and a deep well of empathy and respect for the complexities of human lives and relationships. By approaching these areas with care and ethical consideration, you can honor your ancestors' stories while protecting the feelings and privacy of your living relatives.

Following Up and Sharing: Keeping Relatives Engaged

Your interaction with your relatives shouldn't end when the interview is over. Following up and sharing your progress is a courtesy and a way to maintain their engagement, potentially uncover more information, and strengthen family bonds.

1. **Send a Thank You Note:** Within a few days of the interview, send a handwritten thank you note or an email to express your sincere gratitude for their time, their willingness to share their memories, and their valuable contribution to your research.
2. **Share What You've Learned (with Permission):** As you process the interview information and find supporting documents, share relevant findings with your relatives. This shows them how their contributions are helping you build the family history. If you promised to share copies of photos or documents you digitized, do so promptly. Always obtain permission before sharing information about living individuals or sensitive topics.
3. **Ask Follow-Up Questions (Respectfully):** As you analyze the interview and your initial research, you may have follow-up questions based on something they said or a clue you found. Contact them with specific, concise questions. Be mindful of their time and avoid overwhelming them with requests.

4. **Keep Them Updated on Your Progress:** Periodically update your relatives on the overall progress of your family history project. This could be a brief email or a phone call. Tell them about exciting discoveries you've made, even if they are in a different family branch. This keeps them feeling involved and may prompt them to remember additional details.

5. **Share Your Completed Research (When Ready):** When you have compiled a significant portion of your family history, share it with your relatives in a format they can easily access and enjoy (e.g., a printed report, a link to an online tree, a short presentation). This is the culmination of your collaborative effort and a fantastic way to share the fruits of your labor.

6. **Encourage Their Continued Involvement:** Let your relatives know your door is always open to share additional memories or documents they might find. Please encourage them to talk to other family members and share their stories.

7. **Offer to Help Them with Their Research:** If your relatives are interested in doing their family history research, share your knowledge, resources, and tips.

Maintaining contact and sharing your discoveries fosters a sense of shared ownership in the family history project. Your relatives are more likely to continue supporting your efforts and sharing information if they feel valued and see the results of their contributions.

Building these relationships is an ongoing part of being an ancestry detective.

The Information Harvest: Synthesizing Interview Data and Identifying Clues

Once you have completed your interviews and transcribed your recordings and notes, you are left with a rich harvest of information. The next crucial step is to synthesize this data, organize it within your research system, and carefully analyze it to identify clues that will guide future documentary research.

1. **Transcribe and Organize:** If you recorded your interviews, transcribe them accurately. Organize your transcriptions and notes in your dedicated genealogy workspace, linked to the individuals they pertain to. Use your filing system (physical or digital) to store any photos or documents you acquired during the interviews.

2. **Enter Information into Your Family Tree and Research Log:** Begin entering the names, dates, places, and relationship information you gathered into your pedigree charts, family group sheets, or genealogy software. For each piece of information, record the interview as your source in your research log and potentially in your genealogy software's source citation feature.

3. **Synthesize and Compare Information:** If you interviewed multiple relatives, compare their accounts of the same events or individuals. Note any discrepancies or differing perspectives. This

can highlight areas that require further verification with documentary evidence.

4. **Identify Key Clues for Documentary Research:** As you review the interview data, look for clues that will help you find records. These include:

- **Full names and maiden names:** Crucial for searching indexes and records.
- **Approximate birth, marriage, and death dates:** Helps narrow down record searches.
- **Places of residence:** Essential for searching location-based records like census, land, and probate records.
- **Occupations:** Can lead you to specific record types or occupational directories.
- **Religious affiliations:** Points to church records.
- **Places of education:** Can lead to school records.
- **Military service details:** Provides information for searching military records.
- **Names of siblings, spouses, and children:** Helps expand your tree and apply the FAN principle.
- **Migration details:** Clues about when and where ancestors moved.

- **Mentions of specific documents or photos:** Leads for seeking out physical evidence.
- **Family legends and stories:** Provide hypotheses to investigate with records.

5. **Prioritize Your Research Based on Clues:** Based on the clues you've identified, prioritize which individuals or family lines you will focus on following and which record types you will search. Your research log can help you plan these next steps.

6. **Note Areas of Uncertainty:** Identify areas where the interview information is incomplete or contradictory or where your relatives expressed uncertainty. These are prime areas for targeted documentary research.

7. **Connect Oral History with Existing Knowledge:** Compare the interview information with the information you already had from your initial documents and charts. Note where the interview data confirms or contradicts your existing knowledge.

8. **Reflect on the Stories and Narratives:** Beyond the factual clues, reflect on the stories and memories shared. What do they tell you about your ancestors' personalities, values, and experiences? How do they add depth and meaning to the factual details?

The information gathered from your living relatives is the vital starting point for your ancestry detective work. By carefully synthesizing and analyzing this information, you create a roadmap for your documentary research, ensuring that your efforts are focused and productive. These initial conversations provide the human element that will enrich your family history journey every step of the way.

You have completed the crucial first stage of your investigation: gathering information from the living. With these valuable clues, you are ready to move on to the next phase – exploring the world of historical documents and online resources, which we will begin to do in the following chapters. Your journey as an ancestry detective is well and truly underway!

Chapter 3: Organizing Your Ancestral Archives: Taming the Paper Trail

You've begun your ancestry detective work by gathering invaluable information from your relatives. You've captured their stories, collected precious documents, and perhaps even started filling in your initial pedigree charts. Now, as the clues accumulate, a crucial step can make or break your genealogical journey: getting organized.

Think of yourself as the curator of your family's history. Every piece of information you find – a birth certificate, a census entry, a family photograph, a transcribed interview – must be carefully cataloged, stored, and linked to the broader collection. Without a systematic approach, your growing pile of papers and digital files can quickly become chaotic, making it impossible to find what you need, verify your findings, or track your progress. This chapter guides you in building a robust organizational system that will be the backbone of your ancestry detective work.

The Importance of Organization: Preventing Chaos and Ensuring Progress

It might not be the most glamorous aspect of genealogy, but effective organization is fundamental to long-term success and enjoyment in your research. Skipping this step, or putting it off until you feel overwhelmed, is a common mistake that can lead to frustration, duplicated efforts, and ultimately, giving up on your quest.

Why is organization so crucial for the ancestry detective?

1. **Finding Information When You Need It:** As your collection of documents and notes grows, a sound organizational system ensures you can quickly locate specific records or pieces of information. Imagine finding that one census record among hundreds of unfiled papers, or searching through countless downloads on your computer with vague file names. A well-organized system saves you immense time and frustration.

2. **Preventing Duplication of Effort:** Without a clear record of what you've already searched and found, you will likely waste time and money by repeating searches or re-acquiring documents you already possess. Your research log, a key organizational component, is vital for avoiding this.

3. **Evaluating and Analyzing Information:** A well-organized system allows you to easily group related documents and compare information from different sources. This is crucial for critically evaluating evidence, identifying inconsistencies, and drawing accurate conclusions. You can lay out all the records for a

specific individual or family group and see the complete picture.

4. Identifying Gaps in Your Research: By organizing your information by family line, individual, or record type, you can quickly see where the gaps in your knowledge and documentation exist. This helps you identify your "brick walls" and plan your future research more effectively.

5. Maintaining Source Citations: A sound organizational system goes hand in hand with good source citations. You build a credible and verifiable family history by linking your documents and information to their sources. Your organization should make it easy to record and access the source information for every fact you find.

6. Sharing Your Research: If you want to share your family history with others, a well-organized collection of documents and a clear research log make it much easier to present your findings coherently and well-supported.

7. Preserving Your Research: Organizing your physical and digital documents helps ensure their long-term preservation. Proper storage protects physical documents from damage, and organized digital files are easier to back up and manage.

8. Staying Motivated: Working in a tidy and organized environment, where you can easily see your progress and access your information, can help you stay motivated and engaged in your research. Clutter and disorganization can be demotivating.

9. **Saving Money:** Good organization can actually save you money in the long run by avoiding duplicate record purchases and efficiently utilizing free resources.

10. **Building a Lasting Legacy:** Your organized ancestral archives will ultimately be a valuable legacy for future generations. They will inherit not just a family tree, but a well-documented collection of stories and information they can continue to build upon.

Getting organized from the start is an investment of time and effort that will pay dividends throughout your entire genealogical journey. It transforms your collection of clues into a structured and accessible archive, empowering you to be a more effective and successful ancestry detective.

Physical Organization Systems: Files, Binders, and Storage Solutions

Despite the increasing availability of digital records, you will inevitably accumulate physical documents in your genealogical research. These include original family papers, photocopies of records from archives or libraries, printouts of online documents, and handwritten notes. Establishing a system for organizing these physical materials is essential.

Several popular approaches to physical organization exist, and the best system for you will depend on your preference, the volume of documents you anticipate collecting, and the space you have available. The most important factor is consistency within your chosen system.

Here are some standard physical organization systems:
1. **Surname Filing System:**
    - **How it works:** You create a separate file folder or a section in a binder for each prominent ancestral surname you are researching. Within each surname folder, you can further organize documents by individual or generation.
    - **Advantages:** Simple to understand and implement. Good for focusing on specific family lines.
    - **Disadvantages:** Can become cumbersome if you have many documents for a single surname or are researching multiple unrelated families. Documents related to a couple with different surnames might need to be filed in two places or cross-referenced.
2. **Family Group Filing System:**
    - **How it works:** You create a file folder or a section in a binder for each nuclear family (a couple and their children). The folder is typically labeled with the names of the parents.
    - **Advantages:** Keeps all documents related to a specific family unit together,

which is excellent for applying the FAN principle and analyzing family dynamics. (Friends Associates Neighbors genealogy [1] The **FAN principle** is a crucial research methodology in genealogy, especially when encountering a "brick wall" – a point in your research where direct records for an ancestor are missing or contradictory. FAN stands for **Friends, Associates, and Neighbors**.)

- **Disadvantages:** Requires creating a new folder for each couple, which can result in many folders. Documents about an individual's life before marriage must be filed under their parents' family group.

3. **Individual Filing System:**
   - **How it works:** You create a separate file folder or a section in a binder for each individual in your family tree.
   - **Advantages:** Keeps all documents related to a single person together.
   - **Disadvantages:** Can lead to a vast number of folders as your tree grows. Documents related to a family unit must be duplicated or cross-referenced across multiple individual files.

4. **Locality Filing System:**
   - **How it works:** You organize your files by location where your ancestors lived. Within each locality folder, you can further organize by surname or record type.

- **Advantages:** Useful if your research focuses on specific geographical areas or utilizes local archives. Makes it easy to pull all documents related to a particular place.
- **Disadvantages:** Can be challenging if ancestors moved frequently or if you are researching families who lived in many different locations.

5. **Record Type Filing System:**
   - **How it works:** You organize your files by the record type (e.g., Census Records, Vital Records, Military Records, Land Records). You can further organize each record type folder by surname or location.
   - **Advantages:** Good if you focus on extracting information from specific types of records across multiple family lines.
   - **Disadvantages:** Separates documents related to the same individual or family across folders.

Tips for Physical Organization:

- **Use Acid-Free Materials:** To preserve your valuable documents, use acid-free folders, binders, and page protectors. Standard paper and plastics can degrade over time and damage the documents.
- **Label Clearly and Consistently:** Use clear labels on all your folders and binders. Be consistent with your labeling conventions (e.g., always put the surname first).

- **Use a Consistent Filing Order:** Within each folder, decide on a consistent way to order your documents (e.g., chronologically, alphabetically by individual).
- **Consider Archival Sleeves:** For fragile or crucial documents, use archival-quality plastic sleeves for protection.
- **Store in a Stable Environment:** Store your physical archives in a cool, dry place away from direct sunlight and extreme temperature fluctuations. Basements and attics are generally not ideal due to humidity and temperature variations.
- **Cross-Reference (Optional but Helpful):** If you choose a system that separates documents relevant to multiple individuals or families, consider using a cross-referencing system (e.g., a note in one file indicating where a related document is located). Genealogy software can help with this digital cross-referencing.
- **Don't Overstuff Folders:** Use enough folders so that individual folders are not overly full and documents are easy to access without bending or tearing.

Experiment with different systems on a small scale before committing to one for your entire collection. The goal is to create a system that makes sense to you, is easy to maintain, and allows you to find the information you need quickly.

Digital Organization Systems: Folders, Naming Conventions, and Cloud Storage

In today's world, a significant portion of your genealogical archives will likely be in digital format—scanned documents, downloaded records from online databases, digital photos, interview recordings, and genealogy software files. Organizing these digital assets is just as important as organizing your physical papers.

A well-structured digital filing system will prevent your computer from becoming a digital "junk drawer" and ensure you can easily access and back up your valuable research.

1. **Hierarchical Folder Structure:** Create a logical hierarchy of folders on your computer or in your cloud storage service. Start with a main folder for your genealogy research (e.g., "My Family History"). Within this main folder, create subfolders based on your chosen organizational scheme (similar to the physical systems, such as by surname, family group, or locality). You can then create further subfolders within those for different record types (e.g., "Census," "Vital Records," "Photos," "Interviews").
2. **Example Surname Structure:**
   My Family History
   　　Smith Family
   　　　　John Smith (1850-1920)
   　　　　　　Vital Records
   　　　　　　Census Records
   　　　　　　Land Records
   　　　　　　Photos

    Charles Pembroke
     Mary Jones (1860-1930)
      Vital Records
      Census Records
      Photos
    Jones Family
     ...

Example Locality Structure:
  My Family History
    Wales
      Carmarthenshire
       Laugharne
        Smith Family
        Jones Family
       Kidwelly
        Davies Family

3. **Consistent File Naming Conventions:** This is critical for quickly identifying digital files without opening them. Develop a consistent system for naming your files and stick to it. Include key information in the file name to help you identify the document's content.

4. **Recommended Elements for File Names:**
   a. **Surname:** The primary surname associated with the document.
   b. **Given Name(s):** The first name(s) of the individual(s) concerned.
   c. **Document Type:** What the document is (e.g., Birth_Cert, Marriage_Cert, Census, Deed, Will, Photo, Interview).

d. **Date (of the event or document):** Use a consistent date format (e.g., YYYY-MM-DD or YYYY).
   e. **Location (of the event or document):** The place associated with the record.
   f. **Additional Identifiers:** Any other crucial information (e.g., Volume_Page, Roll_Frame, Interviewee_Name).
5. **Example File Names:**
   a. Smith_John_Birth_Cert_1880-04-15_London.pdf
   b. Jones_Family_1900Census_NewYork_ED123_Sheet5A.jpg
   c. Davies_Thomas_Will_1925-07-10_Carmarthenshire.pdf
   d. Photo_SmithFamily_Picnic_1955_Central Park.jpg
   e. Interview_AuntMildred_2024-11-15.mp3
6. **Tips for File Naming:**
   a. Be consistent!
   b. Use underscores or hyphens instead of spaces.
   c. Avoid using special characters that might cause issues on different operating systems.
   d. Start with the surname for easy alphabetical sorting.
   e. Include enough information to identify the file without opening it.
7. **Cloud Storage:** Storing your digital genealogy files in a reputable cloud storage service (like Google Drive, Dropbox, OneDrive, or specialized

genealogy cloud services) offers numerous benefits:

    a. **Backup:** It provides an automatic off-site backup of your valuable research, protecting against data loss due to hard drive failure, fire, or other disasters.

    b. **Accessibility:** You can access your files from multiple devices (computer, tablet, smartphone) with an internet connection.

    c. **Sharing:** Cloud storage makes sharing specific files or folders easier with other family members or researchers.

    d. **Synchronization:** Files are automatically synchronized across your devices, ensuring you always have the latest version.

8. **Choose a cloud storage provider:** with sufficient space and strong security features.
9. **Genealogy Software and Online Trees:** Your genealogy software or online tree platform is a crucial digital organization tool. These platforms allow you to link your digital documents (scans, downloads) to the specific individuals and facts in your family tree, creating a fully integrated system. They also help you organize sources and generate reports.

By implementing a logical folder structure, a consistent file naming convention, and utilizing cloud storage, you will create a robust digital archive that is organized, accessible, and protected.

Managing Your Research Log: Detailed Tracking of Searches and Results

As discussed in Chapter 1, your research log is the detective's notebook, meticulously documenting every step of your investigation. It's not just a place to record what you *found*, but equally important, what you *searched* and *didn't find*. Maintaining a detailed research log is a cornerstone of organized and efficient genealogical research.

Your research log can take various forms:

1. **Physical Notebook:** A dedicated notebook where you manually record each search is simple and accessible, but it can become bulky over time.

2. **Spreadsheet:** Using a program like Excel, Google Sheets, or a similar spreadsheet application allows you to create a structured table with columns for each piece of information you want to record (Date, Ancestor, Record Type, Location, Search Terms, Result, Source Information, Notes). Spreadsheets are easily searchable and sortable.

3. **Genealogy Software Feature:** Many genealogy software programs and online platforms have built-in research logs or research plans that allow you to link searches to specific individuals and goals. This is often the most integrated approach.

Regardless of the format you choose, the key is to be consistent in recording the essential information for every search:

- **Date of Search:** When you performed the search.
- **Ancestor(s) Being Researched:** The individual(s) or family group you were focusing on.
- **Record Type:** The type of record you searched (e.g., 1900 US Federal Census, New York Passenger Lists, Carmarthenshire Parish Registers).
- **Location of Record/Database:** Where you searched (e.g., Ancestry.com, FamilySearch.org, National Archives, Carmarthenshire Archives). Be specific.
- **Search Terms Used:** The names, dates, places, and keywords you entered. Note any variations you tried.
- **Result of Search:** Did you find relevant information?
    - If yes, briefly describe what you found (e.g., "Found John Smith, age 20, living with parents Thomas and Mary"). Note where you saved or filed the document.
    - If no, state that you didn't find anything (e.g., "No entry found for John Smith in this census"). This is just as important as a positive result.
- **Source Citation Information:** Record enough detail to allow you to create a full source

citation later (e.g., database name, image number, volume/page number, microfilm roll number, archival box number).

- **Notes/Analysis:** Any thoughts, observations, or ideas for future research based on this search. Did the record provide new clues? Did it contradict previous information?

Benefits of a Detailed Research Log:

- **Provides a Roadmap:** Your research log shows you where you've been and helps you plan your next move.
- **Documents Negative Searches:** This is crucial for avoiding repetitive work and confirming that a specific source does not hold the necessary information.
- **Facilitates Source Citation:** It provides the raw data you need to create accurate source citations.
- **Helps Break Down Brick Walls:** By showing you all the sources you've checked for a particular ancestor, it helps you identify which avenues have yet to be explored.
- **Demonstrates Due Diligence:** A well-maintained research log signifies thorough and systematic research.

Start your research log with your first search and record every subsequent search. It is a fundamental tool for staying organized and making efficient progress in your ancestry detective work.

Source Citations Made Simple: Why and How to Cite Your Information

Chapter 1 discussed citing your sources as a cornerstone of sound genealogical research. Now that you are beginning to gather and organize information, it's time to put this principle into practice. Accurate source citation is not about being overly academic; it's about ensuring the reliability and verifiability of your family history.

Why Cite Your Sources?

1. **Verification:** Citations allow you and others to easily find and examine the original source of the information, which is essential for verifying the accuracy of your findings.

2. **Evaluation:** Knowing the source helps you evaluate the reliability of the information. A birth date on a birth certificate is generally more reliable than a birth date recalled from memory by a distant relative.

3. **Tracking:** Citations help you track where you found specific facts, making it easier to revisit the source.

4. **Transparency:** When you share your research, providing citations allows others to see the evidence supporting your conclusions and to build upon your work.

5. **Avoiding Plagiarism:** Citing sources gives credit to the creators and custodians of the records you use.

How to Cite Your Sources (The Simple Approach for Beginners):

While there are complex genealogical citation standards (like the one outlined in *Evidence Explained* by Elizabeth Shown Mills), a beginner must not master these immediately. The most important thing is to adopt a consistent system that includes enough information for you (or someone else) to find the source again easily.

For each piece of information you record (a name, a date, a place, a relationship), note where you found it. At a minimum, your citation should include:

- **What the record is:** (e.g., 1900 U.S. Federal Census, England and Wales Civil Registration Marriage Index, Passenger List from the Port of New York).
- **Where you accessed it:** (e.g., Ancestry.com, FamilySearch.org, National Archives at Washington, D.C., Carmarthenshire Archives).
- **Specific identifying information to locate the record:** This will vary depending on the record type and where you accessed it.
  - **For online databases:** Database name, image number, file name, URL (optional, as URLs can change).
  - **For physical records in an archive or library:** Name of the archive/library, collection name, box number, file number, volume number, page number.

- **For published books:** Book title, author, publisher, publication year, page number.

Examples of Simple Citations:
- *From an online census record:* 1900 U.S. Federal Census, New York, New York County, New York City, Enumeration District 123, Sheet 5A, Household 87, entry for John Smith; accessed via Ancestry.com, image 10 of 30.
- *From an online marriage index:* England and Wales Civil Registration Marriage Index, 1837-1915, July-September 1880, Volume 1a, page 123; accessed via FreeBMD (freebmd.org.uk).
- *From a physical birth certificate:* Birth Certificate for Mary Jones, 10 April 1885, Pontypridd Registration District, Glamorgan, Wales, 1885, Volume 11a, page 678. Held by [Name of person who has the certificate].
- *From an interview:* Interview with Aunt Mildred (Smith) Jones, 15 November 2024, in her home in Chicago, Illinois. Notes and audio recording in possession of [Your Name].

Tips for Citing Sources:
- **Be Consistent:** Choose a format and stick to it.
- **Record the Citation Immediately:** As soon as you find information, record its source in your research log or genealogy software. Don't rely on your memory to add citations later.

- **Link Citations to Facts:** In your genealogy software or family group sheets, link each specific fact (e.g., birth date, place of residence) to its source. One document might be the source for multiple facts.
- **Keep Copies of Documents:** Save or make copies of the original documents whenever possible. This allows you to revisit the source if you have questions or need more information.
- **Don't Be Afraid to Be Detailed:** While a simple system is fine for beginners, including more details in your citations will be helpful in the long run.

By regularly citing sources in your research, you build a foundation of credibility for your family history and ensure that your findings can be verified and expanded upon by yourself and future generations.

Evaluating Your Sources: The Genealogical Proof Standard

As you become more experienced as an ancestry detective, you will encounter situations where different sources provide conflicting information, or where the available records are not as straightforward as you would like. This is where the skill of source evaluation comes into play. The Genealogical Proof Standard (GPS) is a methodology used by genealogists to reach sound conclusions based on evidence. While a complete understanding of the GPS is a more advanced topic, understanding its core principles is valuable even for beginners.

The Genealogical Proof Standard consists of five elements:

1. **Reasonably exhaustive research:** You have searched all relevant sources for information about your research question. You haven't stopped looking because you found one record confirming your theory.

2. **Complete and accurate source citations:** Every statement of fact is supported by a clear and complete citation to the source of the information.

3. **Careful analysis and correlation of the information:** You have critically examined each piece of information, considered its reliability, and compared it with all other relevant information you have found. You look for consistencies and inconsistencies.

4. **Resolution of any conflicting evidence:** If sources provide contradictory information, you have attempted to resolve the conflict by carefully evaluating the reliability of each source and the context in which the data was recorded. You don't ignore conflicting evidence; you address it.

5. **A soundly written conclusion based on the weight of the evidence:** Based on your research, analysis, and resolution of conflicts, you conclude your research question. Your conclusion is supported by the preponderance of the evidence, meaning that the available

evidence makes your conclusion the most likely truth.

Applying the Principles of Evaluation as a Beginner:

While you may not be formally writing conclusions that meet the complete GPS, you can apply the principles of source evaluation in your everyday research:

- **Consider the Source Type:** Is the source a primary source (created at the time of the event by someone with firsthand knowledge, e.g., a birth certificate) or a secondary source (created later by someone without direct knowledge, e.g., a published family history)? Primary sources are generally considered more reliable for the facts they were intended to record.
- **Consider the Informant:** Who provided the information in the record? Was it the person directly involved (e.g., the parents on a birth certificate) or someone less likely to have accurate information (e.g., a neighbor providing information for a death certificate)?
- **Consider the Purpose of the Record:** Why was the record created? A birth certificate records birth details accurately, while a census record counts the population, and some details might be less precise.
- **Look for Consistency:** Does the information in this source align with information

from other sources you've found about the same individual or event?

- **Note Discrepancies:** If you find conflicting information, note it in your research log or notes. Don't just choose the information you like best.
- **Think About the Context:** Consider the historical context in which the record was created. Were there reasons why information might be inaccurate or intentionally misleading (e.g., avoiding military service, social stigma)?

You are already engaging in source evaluation by thinking critically about the information you find and considering the sources it comes from. As you gain experience, you will develop a keener eye for assessing the reliability of different types of records and information. Remember, the goal is to build your family history on credible evidence.

Handling Different Document Types: Certificates, Letters, Photos, and More

Your ancestral archives will likely contain various document types, each requiring specific handling and offering different kinds of information. Understanding how to manage and interpret these diverse records is key to unlocking their secrets.

1. **Vital Records (Birth, Marriage, Death Certificates):**

- **Handling:** Store physical copies in acid-free sleeves and folders. Digitize them for easy access and backup.
- **Information:** Provide crucial dates, places, and names of individuals and their parents. Marriage records connect couples; death records can provide birth dates and parents' names.
- **Tips:** Look for details beyond the basic facts, such as occupations, addresses, and informants' names, which can provide clues for further research.

2. **Census Records:**
   - **Handling:** Digital copies are most common from online databases. Organize by census year, location, and potentially by family.
   - **Information:** Offer snapshots of families at specific times, including names, ages, relationships, occupations, birthplaces, and sometimes immigration details.
   - **Tips:** Examine the entire household, not just your direct ancestor. Look at neighbors as well (the FAN principle). Pay attention to details like immigration year or naturalization status.

3. **Photographs:**
   - **Handling:** Store physical photos in archival sleeves and boxes, away from light and temperature extremes. Digitize photos at high resolution.
   - **Information:** Provide visual records of ancestors and family events. It can trigger memories and help identify individuals. Details

in the photo (clothing, background, objects) can provide clues about period and location.
- o **Tips:** Identify everyone in the photo if possible. Note the date and location if known. Store digital copies with descriptive file names and consider adding tags or metadata.

4. **Letters and Diaries:**
   - o **Handling:** Handle physical letters and diaries with care. Store in archival materials. Digitize the pages. Transcribe the contents to make them searchable and easier to read.
   - o **Information:** Offer personal insights into ancestors' thoughts, feelings, daily lives, relationships, and experiences. Can contain names, dates, places, and details not found in official records.
   - o **Tips:** Pay close attention to dates, locations mentioned, and names of people and places. Look for details that corroborate or contradict information from other sources.

5. **Land and Property Records (Deeds, Mortgages, Tax Records):**
   - o **Handling:** Physical copies are often found in county courthouses or archives. Digitize or get copies. Organize by location and potentially by individual or family.
   - o **Information:** Document property ownership and transfers, which can indicate presence in a location, family relationships (e.g., inheritance), and migration patterns. Tax records track individuals over time.

- **Tips:** Understand the legal descriptions of property. Look for names of grantors and grantees, witnesses, and dower releases (which can indicate a spouse).

6. **Probate and Court Records (Wills, Administrations, Lawsuits):**
   - **Handling:** Physical records are often found in courthouses or archives. Digitize or get copies. Organize by individual and date.
   - **Information:** A will names heirs and can reveal family relationships. Administration records detail the settlement of estates. Other court records can provide details about disputes, guardianships, and other legal matters that involved your ancestors.
   - **Tips:** Read the entire document carefully. Look for the names and relationships of all the individuals mentioned. Note dates and details about property or possessions.

7. **Military Records:**
   - **Handling:** Records are often found in national archives or online databases. Organize by individual and conflict/service period.
   - **Information:** Can provide details about service dates, units, ranks, injuries, pensions, and sometimes physical descriptions and family information.
   - **Tips:** Be aware of the different types of military records available for different conflicts and branches of service.

8. **Newspaper Articles (Obituaries, Marriage Announcements, Local News):**

- **Handling:** Digital copies are increasingly available online. Printouts or clippings need careful handling and storage. Organize by individual, date, or location.
- **Information:** Provide details about births, marriages, deaths, social events, and community involvement. Obituaries can be a wealth of family information.
- **Tips:** Be aware that newspaper information is a secondary source and should be verified. Look for the names of relatives and other individuals mentioned.

By understanding the typical information in different document types and adopting appropriate handling and organizational practices, you can effectively manage your growing collection of ancestral records.

Backing Up Your Data: Protecting Your Precious Research

Imagine spending countless hours meticulously researching your family history, gathering documents, transcribing interviews, and building your family tree, only to lose it all due to a hard drive crash, a stolen computer, or a natural disaster. The thought is enough to make any ancestry detective shudder. This is why backing up your data is not optional but essential.

Your genealogical research is a valuable asset, representing your time, effort, and the culmination of your discoveries. Protecting it with a robust backup strategy is paramount.

1. **The 3-2-1 Backup Rule:** A widely recommended backup strategy is the 3-2-1 rule:
    - **3 Copies of Your Data:** Have at least three copies of your research data.
    - **2 Different Storage Media:** Store your backups on at least two different types of storage media (e.g., your computer's hard drive, an external hard drive, cloud storage, USB drives). This protects against the failure of a single type of media.
    - **1 Off-site Copy:** Keep at least one copy of your backup in a physical location different from your primary research location. This protects against local disasters like fire, flood, or theft. Cloud storage automatically fulfills the off-site requirement.
2. **Backup Your Genealogy Software Files:** If you use genealogy software, ensure you regularly back up your database files. Most software programs have a built-in backup function. Save these backup files to an external drive and/or cloud storage.
3. **Backup Your Digital Documents and Photos:** Create a system for backing up your folders containing scanned documents, downloaded records, and digital photos. You can manually copy these folders to an external drive or use backup software that automates this process. Cloud storage is also an excellent option for backing up these files.

4. **Backup Your Research Log and Other Notes:** Whether your research log is a spreadsheet or a digital document, ensure it is included in your backup routine.

5. **Consider Automation:** Manual backups can be easily forgotten. Use backup software or cloud storage services that offer automatic or scheduled backups. This ensures that your data is regularly protected without you remembering to do it manually.

6. **Test Your Backups:** Periodically test your backup system to ensure you can restore your data from the backups. There's nothing worse than thinking you have a backup only to discover it's corrupted or incomplete when you need it.

7. **Be Mindful of Cloud Storage Limitations:** While cloud storage is convenient for backups, be aware of any storage limits or subscription costs. Ensure you have enough space for your growing archive.

8. **Physical Document Preservation:** While not a "data backup" in the digital sense, properly storing your physical documents in archival materials and a stable environment is crucial for long-term preservation. Consider digitizing fragile or unique documents as an added layer of protection.

Developing a consistent backup routine is essential to being a responsible ancestry detective. Knowing that your hard work and valuable discoveries are protected against loss provides peace of mind. Don't wait until disaster strikes – implement a backup strategy today.

# Integrating Interviews and Documents: Connecting Stories with Records

Your journey as an ancestry detective began with the rich, personal stories and memories shared by your living relatives. As you move forward, you will uncover factual information from historical documents. The real power of your research lies in integrating these two types of information, connecting the stories with the records to create a more complete and compelling picture of your ancestors' lives.

Think of the interview information as the initial sketch, and the documentary evidence as the detailed lines and shading filling the portrait.

1. **Use Interview Clues to Guide Document Research:** The names, dates, places, occupations, and stories you gathered from interviews are the crucial keywords and details you will use to search for records in online databases, archives, and libraries. For example, if your aunt mentioned that her grandfather worked in the coal mines in a specific town, you would search for census records, mining records, and local histories for that town that might mention him.

2. **Use Document Findings to Prompt Further Interview Questions:** As you find information in records, it may raise new questions you can ask your relatives about in follow-up conversations. For example, if a census record shows an unexpected person

living with your ancestors, you might ask a relative if they know who that individual was.

3. **Corroborate Interview Information with Records:** Use documentary evidence to verify the facts shared by your relatives. Did the birth certificate confirm the birth date they remembered? Does the marriage certificate match the story of how your grandparents met? Note where the records confirm or contradict the oral history. When there are discrepancies, investigate further to understand why.

4. **Use Stories to Interpret Documents:** Sometimes, a historical document might be dry or difficult to understand. The stories shared by your relatives can provide context and meaning. For example, a letter describing an arduous journey might make a simple passenger list entry more poignant.

5. **Add Narrative to Your Genealogical Data:** As you enter information into your family tree or genealogy software, incorporate the stories and memories from your interviews into each individual's notes or biographical sections. This brings their entries to life beyond just names and dates.

6. **Create a Combined Timeline:** Develop a timeline for each ancestor or family group that includes factual information from documents and details from oral histories. This will help you see the interplay between documented events and personal experiences.

7. **Link Documents to Stories:** In your organizational system, link the digital copies of your documents to the relevant sections of your interview transcriptions or notes. This allows you to easily see the evidence that supports each part of the story.

8. **Identify New Research Avenues from Both Sources:** Interviews and documents will provide clues that lead to further research. Ensure you record these clues in your research log and plan your next steps based on both types of information.

Integrating your interview data with your documentary evidence is where the puzzle pieces start to fit together. It transforms your family history from scattered facts into a rich tapestry of interconnected lives and experiences. This synthesis is continuous as you uncover new information from living relatives and historical records.

Reviewing and Refining Your System: Adapting Your Organization as You Progress

The organizational system you establish at the beginning of your ancestry detective journey is a great starting point, but it doesn't have to be static. As your research grows, you may find that your initial system needs to be adjusted or expanded to accommodate the' increasing volume and complexity of your findings. Regularly reviewing and refining your organization is a sign of a proactive and effective detective.

1. **Periodically Assess Your System:** Set aside time every few months, or whenever you feel your system is becoming cumbersome, to review how your organization is working. Are you easily finding the documents and information you need? Is your research log up-to-date? Are your digital files well-organized?

2. **Identify Pain Points:** Where are you encountering difficulties with your current system? Are you struggling to find specific types of documents? Is your digital folder structure becoming too deep or confusing? Are your physical files overflowing? Identifying these pain points will help you determine what needs to be adjusted.

3. **Consider Adapting Your Filing Structure:** As your research focuses shift or you accumulate a large amount of information in a particular area, you might consider adapting your filing system. For example, if you initially organized by surname but are now heavily focused on the history of a specific town where many ancestral lines lived, a locality-based system might become more efficient for that portion of your research. You don't have to convert your entire system simultaneously; you can adapt specific sections.

4. **Refine Your Naming Conventions:** As you work with different types of digital documents, you may find that your initial file naming conventions need to be refined to

capture the essential information for each record type.

    5. **Explore New Tools or Features:** As your needs evolve, explore whether new genealogy software features, online organizational tools, or physical storage solutions could improve your system. For example, explore photo management software designed for genealogists if you accumulate many digital photos.

    6. **Don't Be Afraid to Make Changes:** It's better to adapt your system as needed than to stick with a system that isn't working. Don't worry about having a "perfect" system; the goal is to have an effective system for *your* research.

    7. **Consult Resources and Other Genealogists:** Read articles or books about genealogical organizations to get new ideas. Talk to other genealogists about their organizational strategies and what works for them.

    8. **Document Your System Changes:** If you make significant changes to your organizational system, note these changes in your research log or a separate document so you remember how your system is structured.

    9. **Integrate New Types of Information:** As you encounter new types of records (e.g., DNA results, newspaper clippings, court documents), consider how you will integrate them into your existing organizational system.

    10. **The Goal is Efficiency, Not Perfection:** Remember that the purpose of an organization is to make your research easier and more efficient.

Charles Pembroke

> Don't strive for an unattainable level of perfection; focus on creating a system that helps you find information, track your progress, and build your family history effectively.

Your organizational system is a living entity that should evolve with your research. By periodically reviewing and refining your approach, you ensure that your system effectively supports your ancestry detective work. This allows you to focus your energy on the exciting task of uncovering your family's past. With a solid organizational foundation, you can delve into the vast world of genealogical records.

Chapter 4: Navigating the Digital Landscape: Essential Online Resources

As an ancestry detective in the 21st century, your most powerful tool, after the stories and documents held by your living relatives, is the internet. The digital age has revolutionized genealogical research, making millions upon millions of records accessible from the comfort of your home. Archives and libraries worldwide have digitized vast collections, and dedicated genealogy websites have created searchable databases that can help you trace your ancestors across continents and centuries.

This chapter will be your guide to navigating this expansive digital landscape. We will explore the major online platforms, highlight valuable free resources, discuss how to search for information effectively, and equip you with the critical skills needed to evaluate what you find online.

The Internet: A Genealogist's Goldmine

Only a few decades ago, tracing your family history often required extensive travel to courthouses, archives, and libraries, spending hours poring over dusty record books and squinting at microfilm. While visiting physical repositories is still a valuable part of advanced research, the internet has dramatically lowered the barrier to entry for beginners and accelerated the research process for everyone.

The internet has become a genealogist's goldmine for several key reasons:

1. **Accessibility to Records:** Millions of historical records have been digitized and made available online. This includes census records, vital records, immigration lists, military records, probate records, and much more. What once required a trip to a far-flung archive can often now be accessed with a few clicks.

2. **Searchable Databases:** Online platforms have indexed many digitized records, allowing you to search for your ancestors by name, date, place, and other keywords. This capability has transformed the research process, making it possible to quickly find potential records of your ancestors among millions of entries.

3. **Online Family Trees and User Contributions:** Millions of people are researching their family history and sharing their findings online in the form of family trees. While these need to be used cautiously (as we will discuss), they can provide valuable clues and connect you with distant relatives researching your shared ancestors.

4. **Archival and Library Websites:** Many archives, libraries, historical societies, and government agencies have websites that provide

information about their collections, online catalogs, digitized records, and research guides.

5. **Genealogy Communities and Forums:** The internet has connected genealogists from around the globe. Online forums, social media groups, and mailing lists allow researchers to communicate with each other, ask for help, share expertise, and collaborate on research.

6. **Educational Resources:** You can find countless websites, blogs, podcasts, webinars, and online courses dedicated to teaching genealogical research techniques and providing historical context.

7. **Maps and Geographical Tools:** Online mapping tools and historical map collections can help you visualize where your ancestors lived, understand geographical features, and explore historical boundaries.

8. **Newspaper Archives:** Digitized historical newspapers provide a rich source of information, including obituaries, marriage announcements, local news, and social notices that can offer insights into your ancestors' lives.

9. **Specialized Databases:** Beyond the major platforms, there are countless specialized online databases focused on specific regions, ethnic groups, record types, or historical events.

10. **Digital Storytelling and Sharing:** Online platforms and tools make it easier than ever to organize, preserve, and share your family history with others through online trees, digital

scrapbooks, and websites.

However, it's also essential to approach the online world with a detective's critical eye. Not everything you find online is accurate, and the sheer volume of information can sometimes feel overwhelming. This chapter will help you navigate this digital landscape effectively, leveraging its power while being mindful of its potential pitfalls. The internet is a powerful tool, but it is just one tool in the ancestry detective's kit.

Major Genealogy Platforms: Ancestry, FamilySearch, Findmypast, MyHeritage

Several large online platforms dominate the genealogical landscape, offering access to vast collections of records and tools for building your family tree. Most of these operate on a subscription model, but they provide access to records that would be incredibly difficult or time-consuming to obtain. FamilySearch is a notable exception, offering its extensive resources for free. Understanding the strengths and weaknesses of these major players is crucial for planning your online research strategy.

1. **Ancestry (ancestry.com):**
    - **Strengths:** One of the largest and most popular genealogy platforms globally. Offers extensive collections of records, particularly strong for the United States, the United Kingdom, Canada, and Australia. Features a massive collection of user-submitted family trees.

The Ancestry Detective

Provides DNA testing services with an extensive database of users, facilitating connections through genetic genealogy. User-friendly interface and powerful search tools. Offers hints pointing you to potential records for individuals in your tree.

- **Weaknesses:** Subscription can be relatively expensive, with different tiers offering access to different record collections. The quality of user-submitted trees varies widely.
- **Records Include:** Census records, vital records, immigration and passenger lists, military records, probate records, city directories, newspapers, and more.

2. **FamilySearch (familysearch.org):**
   - **Strengths:** Operated by the Church of Jesus Christ of Latter-day Saints (LDS Church), FamilySearch is a non-profit organization and offers all of its resources *for free*. Has a vast and growing collection of digitized records from around the world, with particularly strong coverage for the United States, Canada, and many European and Latin American countries. Features a collaborative "Family Tree" where users contribute to a single, shared tree of humanity (with privacy for living individuals). Offers free online courses and research wikis.
   - **Weaknesses:** The collaborative tree model can sometimes lead to inaccuracies if users add incorrect information without proper sourcing (though the platform is designed to allow for corrections and discussions).

Searching some record collections can be less intuitive than on commercial sites.
- **Records Include:** Billions of digitized images and indexed records, including census records, vital records, church records, land records, probate records, and more. Their collection continues to expand rapidly.

3. **Findmypast (findmypast.com):**
     - **Strengths:** Particularly strong for records from the United Kingdom and Ireland, including extensive collections of parish registers, census records, and military records. Also has growing collections for the United States, Australia, and other countries. Offers historical newspaper archives. Provides DNA testing services.
     - **Weaknesses:** Focus is primarily on the UK and Ireland, so its collections for other regions may be less comprehensive than Ancestry or FamilySearch. Subscription required for full access.
     - **Records Include:** UK and Irish census records, parish registers, military records, passenger lists, newspapers, and more.

4. **MyHeritage (myheritage.com):**
     - **Strengths:** Strong international focus with significant record collections for Europe and other parts of the world, in addition to the United States and the UK. Features a large database of user-submitted family trees. Offers DNA testing services with a global user base, excellent for finding relatives in different countries. Provides tools for creating family tree

charts and reports. Known for its photo enhancement and animation features (e.g., Deep Nostalgia).

- **Weaknesses:** Record coverage can vary by region. Subscription required for full access.
- **Records Include:** Census records, vital records, immigration records, newspapers, and a strong emphasis on European records.

Choosing the Right Platform(s):

As a beginner, FamilySearch is an excellent place to start because it is free and has a vast collection of records and educational resources. You can build your tree, explore their digitized documents, and learn the basics without cost.

If your ancestors are primarily from the United States, Ancestry is often a go-to for its extensive US record collections and large user base. If your roots are heavily in the UK or Ireland, Findmypast will likely be particularly valuable. MyHeritage can be useful for European research and connecting with relatives globally through DNA.

Many experienced genealogists use subscriptions to multiple platforms to access different record sets. However, as a beginner, start with one or two that align with your primary research focus and gradually explore others as your needs and budget allow. Look for free trials to test different platforms before committing to a subscription. Also, check if your local library offers free access to these platforms through their patrons' accounts.

Exploring Free Databases and Websites: A Wealth of Accessible Information

While the major subscription sites offer unparalleled access to many records, there is also a vast and valuable world of free online databases and websites available to the ancestry detective. These resources can complement your research on the major platforms and sometimes hold unique collections unavailable elsewhere.

1. **FamilySearch (Again!):** It's worth reiterating that FamilySearch is the most significant free online resource for genealogical research globally. Its vast collection of digitized records and collaborative Family Tree is invaluable.
2. **Government Archives and Libraries:**
    - **National Archives:** Many countries have national archives with websites that provide information about their holdings, online catalogs, and increasingly, digitized records. Examples include the National Archives of the United States (NARA), The National Archives (UK), and Library and Archives Canada.
    - **State and Provincial Archives:** Individual states (in the US) and provinces (in Canada) often have their archives with online resources and record indexes relevant to that specific region.
    - **Public Libraries:** Many public libraries offer access to subscription genealogy databases (like Ancestry Library Edition, which is

free to use from within the library or sometimes remotely with a library card) and have digitized local history collections, newspapers, and yearbooks.

3. **USGenWeb and WorldGenWeb (usgenweb.org, worldgenweb.org):** These volunteer-driven projects provide websites for individual counties, states, and countries. They often host transcribed records, local histories, cemetery listings, and contact information for local researchers and historical societies. The quality and content vary widely depending on the volunteers involved, but they can be a treasure trove of local information.

4. **Find a Grave (findagrave.com) and BillionGraves (billiongraves.com):** These websites contain millions of cemetery records and gravestone photos uploaded by volunteers worldwide. They can provide birth and death dates, burial locations, and sometimes information about family members buried nearby.

5. **Online Historical Newspaper Archives:** Many libraries, historical societies, and independent websites host digitized collections of historical newspapers. These can be invaluable for finding obituaries, marriage announcements, local news, and other mentions of your ancestors. Some newspaper archives require subscriptions, but many are free to access.

6. **Cemetery Websites:** Many individual cemeteries have their own websites with burial indexes and information.

7. **Ethnic and Religious Archives:** Organizations dedicated to specific ethnic groups or religious

denominations often have archives and online resources relevant to their members.

8. **University and College Archives:** University archives may hold collections related to prominent local families, businesses, or historical events.

9. **Cyndi's List (cyndislist.com):** While not a database, Cyndi's List is a massive, categorized index of online genealogical websites. It's an excellent resource for finding sites related to specific locations, record types, or ethnic groups.

10. **Google and Other Search Engines:** Don't underestimate the power of a simple web search! Use search engines to find information about ancestors, places, or historical topics. Try searching for "[Ancestor's Name] + [Place]" or "[Surname] + [Town] + history."

Exploring these free resources is a crucial part of a comprehensive research strategy. They can provide unique information, help you verify findings from paid sites, and are an excellent option if you are researching on a limited budget. Record the free websites you find most useful in your research log.

Understanding Digitized Records: What's Available and How to Access It

The backbone of online genealogical research is the vast collection of digitized historical records. These are essentially digital images or copies of original documents. Understanding what kinds of records have been digitized and how to access them effectively is key to finding your ancestors online.

What kinds of records have been digitized? Almost every type of historical record imaginable has been digitized by various institutions and organizations:

- **Vital Records:** Birth, marriage, and death certificates and registers.
- **Census Records:** Population schedules from national and local censuses.
- **Immigration Records:** Passenger lists, naturalization records, border crossing records.
- **Military Records:** Service records, pension files, draft registration cards.
- **Probate Records:** Wills, administrations, inventories, court proceedings related to estates.
- **Land and Property Records:** Deeds, grants, tax records.
- **Church Records:** Baptism, marriage, and burial registers from various denominations.
- **Cemetery Records:** Burial indexes, gravestone photos.
- **Newspapers:** Historical newspapers, often keyword-searchable.
- **City Directories and Voter Lists:** Can place ancestors in specific locations at particular times.
- **School, University, and Employment Records:** Details about education and work.
- **Court and Criminal Records:** Information about legal proceedings.
- **Orphanage and Institutional Records:** Records of individuals in care.

- **Photographs, Letters, and Diaries:** Personal collections that have been digitized.
- **Maps and Gazetteers:** Historical maps and geographical dictionaries.

Accessing Digitized Records:

Digitized records are typically accessed through:

1. **Major Genealogy Platforms (Subscription and Free):** As discussed, sites like Ancestry, FamilySearch, Findmypast, and MyHeritage host massive collections of digitized records with searchable indexes.
2. **Archival and Library Websites:** Many national, state, and local archives and libraries have digitized portions of their collections and made them available on their websites.
3. **Historical Society Websites:** Local historical societies often have digitized collections relevant to their specific area.
4. **Specialized Websites and Databases:** Numerous websites focus on specific types of records (e.g., a site dedicated to digitizing passenger lists for a particular port) or specific regions.

Working with Digitized Records:

- **Understand the Index:** Many digitized record collections have an index that allows you to search by name or other keywords. However, indexes can contain errors due to transcription mistakes or difficulty in reading old handwriting. If you can't find your ancestor in the index, try searching with variations of their name, or browse the images directly if the collection is not fully indexed.

- **View the Original Image:** Whenever possible, view the digitized image of the original document, even if you found the information in an index. The original record may contain additional details not included in the index, or you may spot other family members or associates on the same page.
- **Learn to Read Old Handwriting:** Historical documents often feature handwriting that can be challenging to read. Practice deciphering different styles of script from various periods. Many online guides and tutorials are available to help you develop this skill.
- **Understand the Record's Format and Terminology:** Each type of record has its format and uses specific terminology. Familiarize yourself with the typical layout and language of the records you search.
- **Note the Source Information:** When you find a relevant digitized record, carefully note the complete source citation information so you can easily find it again and properly document it in your research log and genealogy software. Include details like the database name, the specific collection, the image number, and other identifying information the platform provides.
- **Save and Organize Digital Copies:** Download or save copies of the digitized records you find and organize them systematically in your digital filing system with clear file names (as

discussed in the previous section).

Digitized records have made genealogical research significantly more accessible. Understanding what types of records are available online and how to access and work with them effectively will substantially expand your ability to uncover your family's past.

Utilizing Online Trees and User-Submitted Information: Promises and Perils

Online family trees and user-submitted information, such as profiles and shared documents on genealogy platforms, represent a massive pool of potential clues and connections. Millions of researchers have contributed their findings, and you may find trees that include your ancestors, potentially extending your known family lines significantly. However, this is an area where the ancestry detective must exercise caution and critical evaluation.

The Promises:

1. **Quick Discovery of Potential Ancestors:** Finding an online tree that includes your ancestors can rapidly expand your family tree, offering names, dates, and places you might not have discovered yet.

2. **Connecting with Distant Relatives:** Online trees can lead you to connect with other researchers who share your ancestors. Collaborating with distant cousins can be incredibly rewarding and lead to sharing information and resources.

3. **Discovering Potential New Lines of Inquiry:** Seeing how others have researched shared ancestors can give you ideas for new records to search or new family lines to explore.

4. **Access to Photos and Documents:** Users often upload photos and digitized documents to their online trees, which can be invaluable additions to your collection (always seek permission to use or share these).

The Perils:

1. **Inaccuracy and Errors:** The most significant peril of online trees is the potential for inaccuracies. Information is often copied from other trees without verification, perpetuating errors. Users may not have followed sound genealogical principles or relied on unreliable sources.

2. **Lack of Source Citations:** Many online trees lack proper source citations, making verifying where the information came from impossible. This is a major red flag.

3. **Assumption-Based Connections:** Some trees may contain connections between individuals based on assumptions rather than documented evidence (e.g., assuming two people with the same surname in the same town are related).

4. **Privacy Concerns:** Users may inadvertently or intentionally include private information about living individuals.

5. **"Gedcom Bombing":** In the past, some researchers would import large, unsourced

GEDCOM files (a standard file format for genealogy data) into online trees, rapidly expanding them with potentially inaccurate information.

Utilizing Online Trees Effectively and Ethically:

- **Treat Online Trees as Hints, Not Facts:** Never accept information from an online tree as definitively accurate without verifying it with sources.
- **Look for Source Citations:** Prioritize online trees that include source citations. Even then, try to examine the cited sources to ensure they support the claims made in the tree.
- **Contact the Tree Owner:** If you find a tree that includes your ancestors, consider contacting the tree owner. Introduce yourself, explain your connection, and ask about their sources for the information. This can open the door to collaboration.
- **Don't Copy and Paste Blindly:** Resist the urge to simply copy information from another user's tree into your own without verification. This is how errors are propagated.
- **Be Mindful of Privacy:** When building your online tree, ensure that the privacy settings are configured to protect information about living individuals. Obtain permission before including or sharing details about living relatives.

- **Document Where You Found the Information:** If you find a clue in an online tree that leads you to a record, cite the *record* as your source, not the online tree itself. You can note in your research log that you found the lead in a specific user's tree.
- **Be Prepared for Disappointment:** You may find trees that seem promising but may be inaccurate or poorly sourced. This is part of the process.
- **Consider Contributing Your Own Well-Sourced Research:** Once you are confident in the accuracy of your research and have proper source citations, consider making your tree public (with privacy for living individuals) to help other researchers.

Online trees can be a valuable tool for discovering clues and connecting with relatives, but they require a critical and cautious approach. Always prioritize verifying information with original, reliable sources.

Beyond the Big Names: Exploring Archival Websites, Library Catalogs, and Historical Societies Online

While the major genealogy platforms offer broad access to popular record sets, smaller institutions like local archives, libraries, and historical societies hold a significant amount of valuable genealogical information. Many of these organizations have an increasing online presence, offering catalogs, finding aids, and even digitized collections unavailable on larger commercial sites.

Exploring these "beyond the big names" resources can often help you overcome obstacles and uncover unique local records.

1. **County and Local Archives:** These repositories hold records specific to a particular county or region, such as local court records, property records, tax lists, and sometimes early vital records before statewide registration. Many have websites about their collections, hours, and contact information. Some are digitizing records and making them available online or through online catalogs.

2. **Public Libraries:** Local public libraries are often treasure troves of local history and genealogical resources. Their websites may offer access to local newspaper archives, digitized yearbooks, city directories, and sometimes even free access to subscription genealogy databases (like Ancestry Library Edition). Their online catalogs can help you find local history books and other relevant materials.

3. **State and Regional Libraries:** These larger libraries often have extensive genealogy and local history collections, including published family histories, rare books, and manuscript collections. Their online catalogs are essential for discovering these resources.

4. **Historical Societies:** Local, regional, and national historical societies are dedicated to preserving and promoting history. Their websites

often provide information about their collections, publications, events, and sometimes have online databases or digitized materials. They can also be excellent places to connect with other researchers interested in the same area.

5. **University and College Archives:** Universities often have archives that hold collections related to the institution's history, prominent alumni, or local families and businesses. Their websites and online catalogs are the best ways to explore their holdings.

6. **Special Collections:** Libraries and archives often have "special collections" that may include unique manuscript collections, diaries, letters, or photographs relevant to local or family history.

7. **Online Catalogs and Finding Aids:** Even if a repository hasn't digitized its records, its online catalog and finding aids (documents describing archival collections' contents) can be incredibly valuable. They help you understand what records exist and where they are located, guiding you to plan future visits or request copies.

8. **Digitized Local Records on Smaller Platforms:** Sometimes, smaller organizations or individuals have digitized specific local record sets and made them available on independent websites. These can be harder to find but are often highly valuable for particular research questions.

Tips for Exploring These Resources:

- **Identify the Relevant Locations:** Determine the counties, towns, and regions where your ancestors lived.
- **Search Online for Local Repositories:** Use search engines to find the websites of the archives, libraries, and historical societies in those locations. Search for terms like "[County Name] archives," "[Town Name] public library genealogy," or "[State Name] historical society."
- **Explore Their Websites Thoroughly:** Look for sections on genealogy, local history, collections, online catalogs, and digitized resources.
- **Check Their Online Catalogs:** Even if there are no digitized records, the catalog will tell you what physical records they hold.
- **Look for Contact Information:** The website should provide contact information if you have specific questions about their collections or need to request copies of records.
- **Be Specific in Your Searches:** When using online catalogs, be specific with names, dates, and places to narrow down your results.

Exploring the websites of these smaller institutions can provide access to unique local records and resources that may hold the key to breaking down your brick walls. They are an essential part of a thorough online research strategy.

Effective Searching Techniques: Keywords, Wildcards, and Filtering Results

Finding your ancestors in the vast online databases requires more than just typing a name into a search box. Becoming proficient in effective searching techniques will significantly increase your success rate and save you time and frustration.

1. **Start Broad, Then Narrow Down:** Begin your searches with the most basic information you know (e.g., a surname and a general location). If you get too many results, add more specific information (e.g., a first name, an approximate birth year). If you get too few results, remove some of the particular criteria.
2. **Use Name Variations:** Note that names were often spelled inconsistently in historical records due to literacy levels, accents, and recording errors. Search for common variations of your ancestor's surname and given name. Use resources like the Soundex system (a phonetic indexing system) or online tools that suggest name variations.
3. **Utilize Wildcards:** Many online databases allow you to use wildcard characters in your search terms to account for variations in spelling. Common wildcards include:
    - * (asterisk): Represents zero or more characters. (e.g., Sm*th would find Smith, Smyth, Smythe).

- ? (question mark): Represents a single character. (e.g., Sm?th would find Smith, Smyth). Check the specific help section of your database to see which wildcards are supported.

4. **Use Quotation Marks for Exact Phrases:** If you are searching for a specific phrase (e.g., a full name like "John Smith" or a place name like "New York City"), enclose it in quotation marks to ensure the search engine looks for that exact phrase.

5. **Understand Search Filters:** Most online databases offer filters that allow you to narrow down your search results by criteria such as:
   - **Year Range:** Limit results to a specific time period.
   - **Location:** Filter by country, state, county, or town.
   - **Record Type:** Limit results to specific records (e.g., census, vital records).
   - **Keywords:** Search for specific words or phrases within the records (e.g., an occupation, a place of origin). Use these filters strategically to refine your search results.

6. **Search by Location First:** If you know where your ancestor lived at a particular time, try searching by that location first and then browse the records for individuals with your ancestor's surname. This can be helpful if the name is

common or you are having trouble finding them through a name search.

7. **Search for Associates and Neighbors:** If you are having trouble finding a direct ancestor, try searching for their known family members, associates (from interviews or other records), or neighbors in the duplicate records and location. They may appear on the same page or in related entries.

8. **Don't Be Afraid to Browse:** If a record collection is not fully indexed, or if you suspect the index contains errors, consider browsing the images directly, page by page. This can be time-consuming, but it can sometimes reveal ancestors that a search missed.

9. **Keep a Record of Your Searches:** Use your research log to record the search terms you used, the databases you searched, and the results. This will prevent you from repeating unsuccessful searches and help you remember what you've already tried.

10. **Read the Database Description:** Before searching a database, read its description carefully. Understand what records are included, the time period covered, and any limitations or quirks of the database or its index.

Becoming a skilled online searcher is an ongoing process. Experiment with different search techniques, utilize the filters and wildcard options available, and keep track of your searches in your research log. You will become more adept at finding your ancestors in the digital landscape with practice.

Evaluating Online Information: Critical Analysis of Digital Sources

Just as you critically evaluate the information shared by your living relatives, it is even more important to critically assess the information you find online. The internet is a powerful tool and a breeding ground for misinformation, transcription errors, and poorly researched family trees. Applying a critical eye to online sources is essential for building an accurate family history.

1. **Consider the Source's Reliability:**
    a. **Original Records vs. Transcribed or Indexed Data:** A digitized image of an original record (like a census page) is generally more reliable than a transcription or index of that record, as transcription errors can occur. Whenever possible, view the original image.
    b. **Government or Institutional Websites vs. Personal Websites:** Information from official government archives, libraries, or reputable historical societies is generally considered more reliable than information on personal websites or blogs (unless the personal site clearly cites its sources).
    c. **Primary vs. Secondary Sources:** Apply the principles of the Genealogical Proof Standard (Chapter 3). Give more weight to

primary sources (created at the time of the event) found online than to secondary sources (interpretations or summaries of primary sources).

2. **Look for Source Citations (and Evaluate Them):** If a website or online tree provides source citations, examine them. Are they specific enough to allow you to find the original source? Are the cited sources reliable? A citation to "Family Bible" is less verifiable than a citation to a specific census record with volume and page numbers.

3. **Identify Potential for Error:** Be aware of the potential for errors in online databases and indexes due to:

    a. **Transcription errors:** Difficulty in reading old handwriting can lead to mistakes when records are transcribed or indexed.

    b. **Scanning errors:** Poor quality scans can make records illegible.

    c. **Indexing limitations:** Not all fields in a record may be indexed.

    d. **Outdated information:** Websites may not be regularly updated.

4. **Compare Information from Multiple Sources:** Never rely on a single online source to confirm a fact. Look for corroborating evidence from other independent sources. If multiple reliable sources agree, you can have more confidence in the information. If sources conflict, investigate further and apply the principles of resolving conflicting evidence.

5. **Be Skeptical of Unsourced Information:** Treat any information found online that does not include a source citation with extreme skepticism. Do not add unsourced details to your family tree as a proven fact.
6. **Evaluate Online Family Trees Critically:** As discussed, online trees should be treated as hints. Look for well-sourced trees whose owners are responsive and willing to share information about their research.
7. **Understand the Website's Purpose:** Is the website's purpose to provide accurate historical records, or is it a platform for users to share their research? Understand the nature of the website and its potential biases or limitations.
8. **Look for "About Us" or "Contact Us" Sections:** Reputable websites providing genealogical information will typically have clear information about their organization, mission, and how to contact them.
9. **Be Aware of Commercial Bias:** Subscription websites have a commercial interest in providing records and tools. While they offer valuable resources, their primary goal is to attract and retain subscribers.
10. **Trust Your Instincts (but Verify):** If something in an online record or tree seems questionable or too good to be true, it might be. Note your concerns and prioritize verifying that information with other sources.

The Ancestry Detective

Developing strong critical thinking skills is essential for navigating the online genealogical landscape. You can build a more accurate and trustworthy family history by questioning the information you find, evaluating its source, and seeking corroborating evidence.

Online Communities and Forums: Connecting with Other Researchers

One of the most valuable aspects of online genealogy is connecting with a global community of fellow researchers. Online forums, social media groups, and mailing lists provide platforms for asking questions, sharing knowledge, collaborating on research challenges, and celebrating discoveries.

1. **Genealogy Forums:** Many large genealogy websites (like Ancestry and FamilySearch) have forums where users can post questions, share tips, and connect with others researching similar surnames or locations. Independent genealogy forums are also dedicated to specific regions, ethnic groups, or research topics.

2. **Social Media Groups:** Facebook and other social media platforms host countless genealogy groups focused on specific surnames, geographical areas, historical periods, or research methods. These groups can be very active and provide a great way to connect with others.

3. **Mailing Lists:** While perhaps less popular than once, genealogical mailing lists focused on specific topics or locations still exist and can be valuable.

4. **Special Interest Groups (SIGs):** Many genealogical societies have online SIGs focused on specific research areas.

5. **Connecting with Online Tree Owners:** As mentioned earlier, contacting the owners of online trees that intersect with your research can lead to valuable connections and information sharing.

Benefits of Engaging with Online Communities:

- **Getting Help with Brick Walls:** Other researchers may have encountered similar challenges and can offer advice or suggest new resources.
- **Learning New Techniques:** Observing discussions and asking questions can help you learn new research strategies and tools.
- **Finding Relevant Resources:** Community members may share information about lesser-known databases, archives, or local resources.
- **Collaborating on Research:** You may find distant relatives researching your shared ancestors, leading to collaborative efforts.
- **Sharing Your Expertise:** As you gain experience, you can contribute to the community by helping others.
- **Motivation and Support:** Connecting with fellow genealogists can provide motivation and support during challenging research periods.
- **Discovering Unexpected Connections:** You might connect with relatives you didn't know existed.

Tips for Engaging with Online Communities:

- **Be Respectful and Polite:** Follow the rules and guidelines of the forum or group. Treat others with respect, even if you disagree.
- **Introduce Yourself:** When joining a new group, consider introducing yourself and your research interests.
- **Be Specific in Your Questions:** When asking for help, provide as much detail as possible about the ancestor you are researching, the information you already have, and the sources you have checked. This makes it easier for others to help you.
- **Cite Your Sources:** When sharing information or asking questions about specific individuals, include the sources for the information you provide.
- **Offer Help When You Can:** As you gain experience, contribute to the community by answering questions or sharing resources related to your areas of expertise.
- **Be Mindful of Privacy:** Do not share private information about living individuals without their consent.
- **Verify Information from Others:** While community members can provide valuable leads, always try to verify information with sources.

Engaging with online genealogy communities can significantly enhance your research journey, providing support, knowledge, and connections that can help you uncover your family's past.

Charles Pembroke

Staying Up-to-Date: Following Genealogy Blogs, Podcasts, and Newsletters

The world of online genealogy is constantly evolving. New records are digitized, new databases are created, and new research techniques are developed. Staying informed about these changes and advancements is crucial to being an effective ancestry detective.

1. **Genealogy Blogs:** Many experienced genealogists, professional researchers, and genealogical organizations maintain blogs where they share research tips, announce new record releases, discuss historical context, and share case studies. Find blogs focusing on the geographical areas or record types you are researching.
2. **Genealogy Podcasts:** Podcasts offer a convenient way to learn about genealogy while commuting, exercising, or doing other tasks. Many podcasts feature interviews with experts, discussions about research techniques, and stories of genealogical discoveries.
3. **Newsletters from Genealogy Platforms and Organizations:** Major genealogy platforms (Ancestry, FamilySearch, etc.) and genealogical societies often send newsletters announcing new record collections, website features, and educational opportunities. Subscribe to newsletters relevant to your research interests.
4. **Social Media:** Follow genealogy experts, organizations, and hashtags on social media platforms

like Twitter, Facebook, and Instagram to stay updated on news and trends.

5. **Online Webinars and Conferences:** Many genealogy organizations and websites offer online webinars and virtual conferences on various topics. These are excellent opportunities to learn from experts and stay current with best practices.

6. **Online Genealogy News Websites:** Some websites report news and developments in the genealogy world, including new record releases and technological advancements.

Benefits of Staying Up-to-Date:

- **Discovering New Records:** Learn about newly digitized collections containing information about your ancestors.
- **Learning New Techniques:** Stay informed about the latest research methodologies and tools.
- **Understanding Historical Context:** Gain deeper insights into the historical periods and places where your ancestors lived.
- **Identifying Relevant Resources:** Learn about new websites, databases, or archives that can help with your research.
- **Staying Motivated:** Hearing about others' discoveries can inspire and motivate you in your own research.

Make it a habit to regularly check in with a few trusted genealogy blogs, podcasts, or newsletters that align with your research interests. Dedicating even a small amount of time each week to staying informed will significantly enhance your skills and increase your chances of making exciting discoveries in your ancestry detective work.

Navigating the digital landscape is an essential skill for the modern ancestry detective. By understanding the major platforms, exploring free resources, employing effective search techniques, critically evaluating online information, engaging with online communities, and staying up-to-date with new developments, you can unlock a vast world of records and information that will help you piece together the compelling story of your family's past. With your organizational system in place (Chapter 3) and your understanding of the digital world expanding, you are now ready to delve into the specifics of different record types, which we will begin to do in the following chapters.

Chapter 5: Decoding Vital Records: Births, Marriages, and Deaths

As an ancestry detective, you are building a case, piece by piece, to prove the identities and relationships of your ancestors. While the stories and memories from your living relatives provide invaluable clues and color, the most fundamental building blocks of your genealogical structure are often found in vital records: records of births, marriages, and deaths. These official documents are the cornerstones upon which you will build a reliable family tree, providing concrete evidence of key life events and individual relationships.

This chapter will delve into the world of vital records, explaining why they are so crucial, what kind of information you can expect to find in them, where to access them, and how to interpret them effectively. Mastering the use of vital records is an essential skill for every ancestry detective.

The Cornerstones of Genealogy: Why Vital Records Are Crucial

Vital records are exactly what their name suggests: records of the most crucial events in a person's life. The moment of their arrival (birth), the formation of new family units (marriage), and the confirmation of their passing (death). These records are created by civil or religious authorities to document these events officially, and because of their official nature, they are generally considered highly reliable sources of information.

Why are birth, marriage, and death records the cornerstones of genealogical research?

1. **Proof of Existence:** A birth certificate is official proof that a person was born on a specific date and place. A death certificate confirms that a person died and provides details about their passing.
2. **Establishing Relationships:** Birth certificates typically name the individual's parents. Marriage records name the bride and groom and often their parents, connecting two families. Death certificates may name a spouse or parents. These direct links between individuals are fundamental to building your family tree accurately.
3. **Providing Key Dates and Places:** These records provide the essential dates and places that form the timeline and geographical framework of your ancestors' lives. Knowing a birth date and place allows you to estimate an age for census searches. Knowing a marriage date and place helps you find the marriage record itself and potentially church records. A death date and place can lead to burial records, obituaries, and probate records.
4. **Guiding Further Research:** The information in vital records often provides clues that lead you to other types of records. For

example, a birth certificate might list a father's occupation, which could lead you to employment records or city directories. A death certificate might list a spouse's name, which confirms a marriage. A birthplace listed on a marriage or death certificate can guide your research to a new location.

5. **Verifying Other Information:** Information found in vital records can be used to verify or clarify information found in less reliable sources, such as family stories, online trees, or other historical documents that may contain approximations or inaccuracies.

6. **Understanding Historical Context:** Examining vital records over time can reveal changes in naming conventions, social customs (like age of marriage), migration patterns, and even common causes of death, providing insights into the historical context of your ancestors' lives.

7. **Legal and Official Documentation:** These records were created for legal and administrative purposes, making them generally more standardized and consistently kept than other historical records.

8. **Often Indexed and Accessible:** Due to their importance, vital records are frequently among the first types of records to be indexed and digitized by genealogical organizations, making them relatively accessible for online searching.

While not every ancestor will have easily locatable vital records (especially in earlier periods or certain regions), when available, they provide the most direct and reliable evidence for establishing key facts and relationships in your family history. They are the foundational documents that will give your family tree structure and credibility.

Birth Records: Information on Individuals and Parents

A birth record is the official document created to record a child's birth. The level of detail in birth records has evolved significantly over time. It varies by location, but they are consistently one of the most valuable sources for genealogists, especially for identifying parentage.

Information Typically Found on a Birth Record:

Early birth records, particularly those kept by churches, might be very brief, simply recording the child's name, the date of birth or baptism, and the parents' names. However, civil registration records, which became more standardized over time, often contain a wealth of information:

- **Child's Full Name:** Sometimes includes the given name(s) and surname.
- **Date and Time of Birth:** Precise details of when the birth occurred.
- **Place of Birth:** The street address, town, county, and state or country where the birth occurred. This is crucial geographical information.

- **Sex of the Child:** Male or Female.
- **Mother's Full Name:** This usually includes her maiden name. This is often the *only* record that definitively links a child to their mother using her maiden name, which is vital for tracing maternal lines.
- **Father's Full Name:** The full name of the child's father.
- **Parents' Usual Residence:** The place where the parents lived, which may be different from the place of birth.
- **Parents' Ages or Birth Dates:** Can provide an estimate or exact date for the parents' births.
- **Parents' Birthplaces:** Indicates where the parents were born, guiding research to earlier locations.
- **Father's Occupation:** Provides clues about his work and social status.
- **Number of Children Born to the Mother:** Can help distinguish between mothers with the same name.
- **Name of the Person Reporting the Birth:** Often a parent, doctor, midwife, or other witness.
- **Date of Registration:** When the birth was officially recorded.

Finding and Using Birth Records:

- **Civil Registration:** Many countries implemented civil registration of births, marriages, and deaths in the 19th century. In

England and Wales, civil registration began in 1837. In Scotland, it started in 1855 (with more detail initially). In Ireland, it began in 1864 (non-Catholic marriages from 1845). In the United States, the implementation varied by state and county, with many states starting statewide registration in the late 19th or early 20th century.

- **Church Records (Baptisms):** Before widespread civil registration, or in areas where it was not consistently enforced, church baptismal records are often the best source for birth information and parentage. These records typically list the child's name, baptism date (usually shortly after birth), and the parents' names. They may also name godparents or sponsors, often relatives who can provide additional clues.
- **Online Databases:** Major genealogy platforms like Ancestry, FamilySearch, Findmypast, and MyHeritage have extensive collections of digitized birth records and indexes from various countries and periods. FamilySearch has an extensive collection of digitized church records.
- **Government Archives and Offices:** Civil birth records are typically held by state, county, or local government agencies. You may need to contact the relevant vital records office or state archives to request copies of certificates, especially for more recent records, which may not be available online due to privacy restrictions.

- **Abstracts and Indexes:** Online databases often provide indexes or abstracts of birth records. While these are useful for searching, always try to view the original record image if available for the most complete and accurate information.

Tips for Using Birth Records:
- **Prioritize Finding Original Records:** The information on an original birth certificate is generally the most reliable.
- **Note All Information:** Don't just extract the child's name and birth date. Record everything on the certificate; even seemingly minor details can be valuable clues.
- **Pay Attention to the Informant:** The person who provided the information for the birth record is often a parent, which increases the likelihood of the information being accurate.
- **Use the Mother's Maiden Name:** The mother's maiden name on a birth certificate is crucial for tracing her family line.
- **Look for Parents' Birthplaces:** This information can guide your research to an earlier generation and a new location.
- **Consider Naming Patterns:** Sometimes, children's names are repeated in generations or are named after parents, grandparents, or other relatives.
- **Be Aware of Delayed Registrations:** In some cases, births were not registered until

years after the fact, and the information might be less accurate.

Birth records are fundamental to connecting children to their parents and establishing key facts about an individual's entry into the world. They are often the first crucial link in tracing a new generation.

Marriage Records: Proof of Union and Clues to Family Connections

Marriage records document the union of two individuals and are invaluable for connecting families and extending your pedigree sideways and upwards. They provide proof of a relationship between a husband and wife and often offer clues about their origins and parents.

Information Typically Found on a Marriage Record:

Like birth records, the detail in marriage records varies by time and location, but common information includes:

- **Names of the Bride and Groom:** Full names are usually provided.
- **Date of Marriage:** The exact date the marriage took place.
- **Place of Marriage:** The church, town, county, and state or country where the ceremony occurred.

- **Ages or Birth Dates of the Bride and Groom:** Can help estimate their birth years and find birth records.
- **Residences of the Bride and Groom:** Indicates where they lived during the marriage.
- **Marital Status Before Marriage:** (e.g., single, widowed, divorced). If widowed, the name of the previous spouse may be included.
- **Names of the Parents of the Bride:** Usually includes the father's full name and the mother's full name (often including her maiden name). This is a key piece of information for identifying the previous generation.
- **Names of the Parents of the Groom:** Similar information for the groom's parents.
- **The occupations of the Bride and Groom (or their Fathers)** provide clues about their work and social standing.
- **Names of Witnesses:** Witnesses were often family members or close friends, providing potential leads for applying the FAN principle.
- **Name of the Officiant:** The person who performed the ceremony (minister, justice of the peace), which can point to church records.
- **Date of License/Banns:** The date the marriage license was issued or the banns (public announcements of intent to marry in a church) were read.

Finding and Using Marriage Records:

- **Civil Registration:** Where civil registration exists, marriage records are typically recorded by the same government agencies that handle births and deaths.
- **Church Records (Registers and Banns):** For periods before or in areas without consistent civil registration, church marriage registers are a primary source. Marriage banns, which were announced in the weeks leading up to a marriage, can also provide information.
- **Marriage Licenses and Bonds:** In some jurisdictions, couples must obtain a marriage license before marrying. Marriage bonds were sometimes posted to guarantee no legal impediment to the marriage. These documents can predate the actual marriage record and may contain additional information.
- **Online Databases:** Major genealogy platforms have extensive collections of digitized marriage records and indexes. FamilySearch has a comprehensive collection of digitized church marriage records.
- **County Courthouses:** Marriage records were often kept at the county level in the United States. Contacting the county clerk's office in the relevant county is usually necessary to obtain copies of records.
- **Parish Chests (UK):** In England and Wales, older parish registers were often kept in a

chest in the church. Many have now been deposited or digitized in county record offices.

- **Marriage Indexes:** Online indexes can help you quickly find potential marriage records, but always try to view the original record image or obtain a copy for complete information.

Tips for Using Marriage Records:

- **Look for Parents' Names:** This is one of the most valuable information on a marriage record for extending your family tree.
- **Note All Details:** Record all the information on the certificate or register, including witnesses and the officiant.
- **Use Marriage Records to Estimate Birth Dates:** The ages provided on a marriage record can help you estimate the birth years of the bride and groom.
- **Pay Attention to Residences:** The residences listed can confirm or provide clues about where the couple lived before and after the marriage.
- **Consider Multiple Marriages:** People often marry more than once. Be sure to investigate potential previous marriages for your ancestors.
- **Be aware of different marriage practices:** Marriage customs and record-keeping vary between denominations.

- **Check for Marriage Bonds or Licenses:** These may exist even if a formal marriage register entry is harder to find.

Marriage records are essential for proving spousal relationships and identifying a married couple's parents, thereby extending your family tree back another generation.

Death Records: Confirming Passing and Revealing Key Details

Death records confirm an individual's passing and often provide valuable information about their life, including their birth date, birthplace, and parents' names. While they record the end of a life, they can open up new avenues for researching that life.

Information Typically Found on a Death Record:

The information on a death record can be a combination of factual details about the death and biographical information about the deceased. Common elements include:

- **Deceased's Full Name:** The name of the person who died.
- **Date and Time of Death:** When the death occurred.
- **Place of Death:** The address, town, county, and state or country where the death occurred.
- **Cause of Death:** The medical reason for the death, which can sometimes provide

historical context about health conditions of the time.
- **Date of Birth:** The deceased's birth date. This is often a crucial piece of information.
- **Place of Birth:** The deceased's birthplace, which can guide research to an earlier location.
- **Age at Death:** Can help estimate the birth year if the birth date is unknown.
- **Occupation:** The deceased's occupation.
- **Marital Status:** (e.g., single, married, widowed, divorced). If married or widowed, the name of the spouse may be included.
- **Name of Spouse:** The name of the surviving or deceased spouse.
- **Names of Parents:** Crucially, the names of the deceased's parents are often included, sometimes including the mother's maiden name. This is incredibly valuable for confirming parentage.
- **Informant's Name and Relationship to Deceased:** The person who provided the information for the death certificate. This is important for evaluating the accuracy of the biographical details; a spouse or child is more likely to have accurate information than a neighbor or institution.
- **Burial or Cremation Information:** Date and place of burial or cremation, and the cemetery's name. This can lead you to cemetery records.

- **Undertaker Information:** Details about the funeral home.
- **Date of Registration:** When the death was officially recorded.

Finding and Using Death Records:

- **Civil Registration:** Death records are part of civil registration systems and are held by state, county, or local government agencies.
- **Cemetery Records:** Cemetery offices and websites often have burial registers and maps that can provide death and burial dates. Websites like Find a Grave and BillionGraves are excellent resources for finding gravestone information.
- **Church Records (Burials):** Church burial registers recorded deaths and burials before civil registration.
- **Funeral Home Records:** Funeral homes may have records of services and burials.
- **Obituaries and Newspaper Death Notices:** Newspapers often published obituaries or brief death notices that can contain significant genealogical information, including names of surviving relatives, biographical details, and burial information. These are valuable secondary sources.
- **Online Databases:** Major genealogy platforms have extensive collections of digitized death records, indexes, and cemetery records.
- **Social Security Death Index (US):** A valuable index of deaths reported to the U.S.

Social Security Administration, primarily for deaths from the mid-20th century onwards. It typically includes name, birth date, death date, and last known residence.

- **Probate Records:** While not strictly death records, probate records (Chapter 10) are created after a person's death and confirm their passing.

Tips for Using Death Records:

- **Look for Birth Date and Place:** If a birth certificate is not available, a death certificate is often the best source for a precise birth date and place.
- **Note Parents' Names:** Including parents' names is a key feature for confirming parentage.
- **Consider the Informant's Reliability:** Evaluate the likely accuracy of the biographical information based on who provided it.
- **Use Burial Information:** The cemetery name and burial date can lead you to cemetery records, which may provide additional details or identify other nearby family members.
- **Search for Obituaries:** Newspapers can provide rich biographical details not found on death certificates.
- **Be Aware of Inaccuracies:** Information on a death certificate about birth date, birthplace, and parents' names is often provided by a surviving relative or informant who may not have had completely accurate information,

especially if the deceased was elderly or had been estranged from family. Corroborate this information with other sources.

Death records serve as a final official marker in an ancestor's life. They can provide crucial links and details for your research, particularly for confirming parentage and identifying spouses and burial locations.

Accessing Vital Records: State, County, and Local Archives

While online databases have made accessing many vital records easier than ever, a significant number of records, particularly more recent ones or those from less widely digitized collections, still reside in physical archives and government offices. Understanding where these records are held and how to access them is essential for comprehensive research.

The location of vital records custody varies significantly depending on the country, state, and time period.

1. **United States:**
    a. **State Level:** Statewide registration of births, marriages, and deaths began at different times in each state, generally in the late 19th or early 20th century. State vital records offices (often part of the Department of Health) are the primary custodians of these records. Access to more recent records (typically within the last 50-100 years) is often restricted due

to privacy laws, and only direct descendants or individuals with a legal right may obtain certified copies. Older records may be transferred to the State Archives and may be more easily accessible or even digitized.
b. **County Level:** Before statewide registration, vital events were often recorded at the county level, typically by the County Clerk or a similar official. Many county courthouses still hold these older records. Some county records have been digitized and made available on platforms like Ancestry, FamilySearch, or county government websites.
c. **City Level:** Vital records may also have been kept at the city level in some major cities.

2. **United Kingdom:**
   a. **England and Wales:** Civil registration began in 1837. Records are held by the General Register Office (GRO). Indexes to these records are widely available online (on subscription sites and free sites like FreeBMD and the GRO's index search). You can order copies of certificates from the GRO or the local Register Office where the event occurred. Parish registers (for events before 1837 and sometimes concurrently) are held in local parish churches or county record offices.

Many parish registers have been digitized and are available on major genealogy platforms.

b. **Scotland:** Civil registration began in 1855. Records are held by the National Records of Scotland (formerly the General Register Office for Scotland). Indexes and digitized images are available on the ScotlandsPeople website (pay-per-view). The National Records of Scotland or local archives also hold older parish registers.

c. **Ireland (Republic of Ireland and Northern Ireland):** Civil registration began in 1864 (non-Catholic marriages from 1845). Records are held by the General Register Office in Dublin and the General Register Office in Belfast. Indexes are available online, and certificates can be ordered. Church records are vital in Ireland due to historical factors.

d. **Other Countries:** Access to vital records varies significantly by country. Researching the specific vital record system for your ancestors' country is essential. Government archives, national libraries, and religious institutions are common custodians of these records.

Accessing Records in Person:

Visiting archives and government offices in person can be a rewarding experience. You can access original records and potentially find documents that are not available online.

- **Plan Your Visit:** Research the repository's holdings, hours of operation, and any visitor requirements (e.g., appointments, identification, rules about pens and scanners).
- **Be Prepared:** Bring your research log, notes about the specific records you seek, and any necessary forms or identification.
- **Utilize Staff Expertise:** Archivists and librarians know their collections and can provide valuable assistance.
- **Be Respectful of Records:** Handle historical documents with care.

Accessing Records Online:

Chapter 4 discusses online databases as a primary method for accessing digitized vital records and indexes.

- **Search Indexes:** Start by searching indexes on major platforms or free websites using variations of your ancestor's name and relevant dates/locations.
- **View Original Images:** If an index entry is found, try to view the digitized image of the original record.
- **Browse Collections:** If an index is unavailable or incomplete, consider browsing

digitized collections page by page, especially for records organized chronologically or geographically.

Understanding the jurisdictional flow of vital records and the various avenues for accessing them, both physically and online, is key to a successful search.

Requesting Records by Mail or Online: Procedures and Tips for Success

If vital records are unavailable online or you need a certified copy, you must request the record from the relevant government office or archive. This process requires understanding the procedures and providing accurate information.

1. **Identify the Correct Office:** Determine which government office holds the record you need. For civil registration records, this is typically a state vital records office (US), the GRO (UK), or a similar agency in other countries. It would be the county clerk's office for older county-level records in the US. For church records, it might be a local church, a diocese, or a denominational archive.

2. **Check Their Website:** Most vital records offices and archives have websites that provide information on requesting records, including eligibility requirements, fees, and necessary forms.

3. **Understand Eligibility and Restrictions:** Access to recent vital records is often restricted to direct descendants or those with a legal right. You may need to provide proof of your relationship to the individual.
4. **Gather Necessary Information:** To request a record, you will typically need to provide as much information as possible about the individual and the event, including:
   - Full name of the individual.
   - Date of the event (exact or approximate).
   - Place of the event (town, county, state/country).
   - Names of parents (for birth records).
   - Names of spouses (for marriage or death records).
   - Any other identifying information you have. The more information you can provide, the easier it will be for the office to locate the record.
5. **Download or Request the Application Form:** Most offices require you to submit a formal application form for a copy of a vital record. These are often available for download on their websites.
6. **Provide Proof of Identity and Relationship (if required):** For restricted records, you will likely need to provide a copy of your identification and documents proving your relationship to the individual whose record you

are requesting (e.g., your birth certificate or your parents' marriage certificate).

7. **Pay the Required Fee:** Requesting copies of vital records typically involves a fee. Check the office's website for the current fee and accepted payment methods.

8. **Submit Your Request:** Mail your completed application, necessary documentation, and payment, or submit it online if that option is available.

9. **Be Patient:** Processing times for vital record requests can vary depending on the office's workload. Be patient and allow sufficient time for your request to be processed.

10. **Keep a Record of Your Request:** Note the date you submitted the request, the information you provided, and the fee paid in your research log.

Tips for Success:

- **Be as Accurate as Possible:** Provide the most accurate information about the individual and the event.
- **Include All Known Variations:** If you know of alternative spellings of names or approximate dates, include them in your request.
- **Explain Your Purpose:** Briefly explain that you are requesting the record for genealogical research.
- **Request an "Informational" or "Uncertified" Copy if Possible:** If you do not

need a certified copy for legal purposes, an informational or uncertified copy is often less expensive and may be easier to obtain, especially for older records.

- **Check for Online Ordering Options:** Many vital records offices now allow you to order copies of records online, which can be faster and more convenient.
- **Contact the Office with Questions:** If unsure about the procedure or what information to provide, contact the vital records office directly.

Requesting vital records from government offices is a common step in genealogical research. You can obtain these crucial documents to build your family history by understanding the procedures and providing accurate information.

Understanding Historical Variations: How Vital Records Have Changed Over Time

As an ancestry detective working with records from different periods, it is essential to understand that the format, content, and even the very existence of vital records have changed significantly over time. What might be considered a standard birth certificate today differs greatly from a baptismal entry in a 17th-century church register.

Here are some key ways vital records have varied historically:

1. **Shift from Religious to Civil Registration:** In many Western countries, the primary responsibility for recording births, marriages, and deaths shifted from religious institutions (churches) to civil authorities (government) in the 19th century. This transition meant more standardized forms, more consistent record-keeping, and often more detailed information collected.

2. **Increasing Detail Over Time:** Early records were often fundamental, containing only the most essential information. Over time, governments and churches began collecting more detailed information on vital records, such as parents' birthplaces, occupations, and the number of previous children born to a mother.

3. **Standardization of Forms:** Early record-keeping was often less standardized, with recorders using their formats and abbreviations. Civil registration brought about more uniform forms and procedures.

4. **Legibility of Handwriting:** The handwriting style has changed dramatically over the centuries. Learning to read older scripts (like various forms of cursive or even earlier hands) is necessary for working with historical vital records.

5. **Language:** Depending on the historical period and location, vital records may be in languages other than English or use archaic terminology and abbreviations.

6. **Record-Keeping Practices:** The diligence and consistency of record-keeping varied greatly depending on the recorder, the institution, and the region's stability. Some periods or locations may have patchy or incomplete records.

7. **Information Collected Based on Social Norms and Laws:** The information considered essential to collect on vital records reflected the social norms and laws of the time. For example, some historical records might include information about race or legitimacy.

8. **Privacy Laws:** Modern privacy laws have restricted access to vital records, particularly more recent ones. Earlier records were often more openly accessible.

9. **Impact of Historical Events:** Wars, natural disasters, and social unrest could disrupt record-keeping or destroy records.

Examples of Historical Variations:

- **Earlier Church Records:** Often brief, handwritten entries in a register, potentially in Latin or an older local language form. May only include names and dates of baptism/marriage/burial.
- **Early Civil Registration (e.g., mid-19th century):** More standardized forms, but potentially fewer details than later records. Handwriting is still a factor.
- **Later Civil Registration (e.g., early 20th century onwards):** More detailed forms with more structured information, often typed or

completed in more modern handwriting.

Being aware of these historical variations is crucial for interpreting vital records accurately. Don't expect a 17th-century baptismal record to resemble a 20th-century birth certificate. Researching the specific history of vital record keeping in the locations and periods you are researching will significantly enhance your ability to find and understand these records.

Interpreting the Information: Deciphering Handwriting, Abbreviations, and Jargon

Once you locate a vital record, the task shifts from finding the document to accurately interpreting its information. This often involves deciphering old handwriting, understanding abbreviations, and recognizing historical jargon.

1. **Deciphering Handwriting:** This is one of the most common challenges when working with historical records. Handwriting styles have significantly changed, and individual handwriting can vary greatly.
    - **Practice:** The best way to improve your ability to read old handwriting is to practice regularly. Start with records where you know some information and use that to help you decipher the rest.
    - **Learn Common Styles:** Familiarize yourself with common historical handwriting styles for your

research periods and locations. Online tutorials and guides are available.

- **Look for Letter Formations:** Pay attention to how individual letters are formed, especially challenging ones like "s," "f," "t," "r," and capital letters.
- **Compare Letters within the Document:** If you can decipher one word, compare the formation of its letters to similar letters in other words in the document.
- **Consider the Context:** The surrounding words and the document type can help you guess unfamiliar words.
- **Look for Abbreviations:** Be aware that abbreviations were commonly used in historical documents.
- **Seek Assistance:** If you struggle to read a document, ask for help from more experienced genealogists or online communities.

2. **Understanding Abbreviations:** Historical records often use no longer standard abbreviations.

- **Common Latin Abbreviations (in older church records):** Be aware of standard Latin abbreviations used in church registers, such as "bp." or "bapt." (baptized), "m." or "mar." (married), "bur." (buried), "fil." (filius - son), "filia" (daughter), "ux." (uxor - wife).

- **Occupational Abbreviations:** Abbreviations for occupations were also standard.
- **Context is Key:** Use the context of the document to help you interpret abbreviations.
- **Consult Reference Guides:** There are online and published guides to historical abbreviations used in genealogical records.

3. **Recognizing Historical Jargon and Terminology:** Historical documents may use words or phrases that have different meanings today or are no longer commonly used.
   - **Occupational Terms:** Be prepared to encounter historical occupational titles that you may not recognize (e.g., "cordwainer" for shoemaker, "farinaceous" for dealing in flour).
   - **Relationship Terms:** Some historical terms for relationships may differ from modern usage (e.g., "cousin" could refer to any relative, not just a first cousin).
   - **Legal and Medical Terms:** Probate records and death certificates may contain legal or medical terminology that requires understanding.
   - **Geographical Terms:** Be aware of historical place names or administrative divisions that may have changed over

time.

4. **Interpreting Dates:** Be mindful of how dates were recorded historically.
    - **Julian vs. Gregorian Calendar:** Understand the transition from the Julian calendar to the Gregorian calendar in the 18th century in some countries, which can affect dates before the changeover.
    - **Quaker Dates:** Quaker records often used numbered months (e.g., "7th month"), which can be confusing if you are unfamiliar with their system.
    - **Regnal Years:** Some older official documents may date events by the regnal year of the monarch.

5. **Evaluating the Informant:** As mentioned earlier, consider who provided the information for the vital record. Their relationship to the individual can affect the likely accuracy of the details provided.

Interpreting historical vital records is a skill that develops with practice and familiarity with different record types and historical contexts. Don't be afraid to examine each document carefully and utilize resources like handwriting guides and dictionaries of historical terms.

Charles Pembroke

Beyond the Certificate: Using Vital Records as Springboards for Further Research

Finding a birth, marriage, or death certificate is a significant milestone, but the information in these documents is often a springboard for further investigation. Vital records rarely provide the complete story of an ancestor's life; instead, they offer clues that can lead you to a wealth of other documents.

Here's how to use the information in vital records to guide your subsequent research:

1. **Names of Parents and Spouses:** This is the most obvious clue. The names provided allow you to extend your family tree to the previous generation (from a birth or marriage record) or identify a spouse (from a marriage or death record). These names become your search terms for finding their vital records, census entries, and other documents.

2. **Birth Date and Place:** These details are crucial for finding your ancestor in census records organized by location and taken at specific intervals. Knowing the birthplace can guide your research to a new geographical area.

3. **Place of Event (Birth, Marriage, Death):** The location where a vital event occurred is essential for searching local records, including land records, probate records, church records, and local histories. It also helps you understand your ancestors' geographical movements.

4. **Occupations:** An occupation listed on a vital record can lead you to city directories, professional directories, union records, or records related to specific industries.

5. **Residences:** Addresses listed on marriage or death records can be used to find ancestors in city directories, tax records, or even to locate historical maps of the area.

6. **Witnesses and Informants:** The names of witnesses on a marriage record or the informant on a death record can be valuable. They were often family members, friends, or neighbors, and researching them (applying the FAN principle) can sometimes provide clues about your direct ancestor.

7. **Burial Information:** The cemetery name and burial date on a death certificate will lead you to cemetery records, which may provide additional biographical details or identify other family members buried nearby.

8. **Cause of Death:** While not always directly genealogical, the cause of death can provide historical context about health conditions and medical practices of the time.

9. **Parents' Birthplaces (if listed):** This is a direct clue that points you to the likely location of your ancestors in the previous generation, guiding your research to a new area.

10. **Marital Status:** Knowing if an ancestor was widowed or divorced can prompt you to look for previous marriages or divorce proceedings

records.

Treat every piece of information on a vital record as a potential clue. Extract all the details, record them accurately in your research log and family tree, and then brainstorm how each detail could lead you to other sources of information about your ancestor's life. Vital records are often the starting point for tracing an ancestor's journey through census records, migration paths, and other life events.

Troubleshooting Missing Records: Alternative Sources When Vital Records Are Unavailable

Despite their importance, you will inevitably encounter situations in your ancestry detective work where vital records for a specific ancestor seem to be missing. This can be due to records being lost or destroyed (by fire, flood, or neglect), poor record-keeping in a particular time or place, or ancestors intentionally avoiding official registration. When you hit this kind of "brick wall," it's time to get creative and explore alternative sources that can provide the same or similar information.

Here are some alternative sources to explore when vital records are unavailable:
1. **Census Records:** Census records often include information about age, birthplace, and relationships within a household. While not as precise as a birth certificate, they can provide valuable estimates and confirm familial

connections at a specific time. Later census records (mid-19th century onwards) often asked for more detailed information like parents' birthplaces and marriage duration.

2. **Church Records (Baptisms, Marriages, Burials):** As mentioned earlier, church records often predate civil registration and can serve as excellent substitutes for birth, marriage, and death records.
3. **Cemetery Records and Gravestone Inscriptions:** Gravestones often include birth and death dates. Cemetery registers may contain additional biographical information and details about who purchased the plot or who else is buried nearby.
4. **Obituaries and Newspaper Articles:** Obituaries can be a rich source of information, often providing birth and death dates and places, names of parents and spouses, surviving relatives, and biographical details. Marriage announcements and other newspaper articles can also provide vital information.
5. **Probate Records (Wills and Administrations):** Wills often name spouses and children, providing evidence of relationships. Estate administration records may also mention heirs and their relationships to the deceased.
6. **Land and Property Records:** Deeds and other land records can sometimes mention relationships (e.g., a deed from a father to a son, or a dower release by a wife).

7. **Military Records:** Military service records, pension applications, and draft registration cards can include information about age, birthplace, and sometimes details about family members.
8. **Bible Records:** Family Bibles were often used to record births, marriages, and deaths within a family. If a family Bible has been preserved, its information can be a valuable (though secondary) source.
9. **Family Letters and Diaries:** Personal correspondence and diaries can mention births, marriages, deaths, and other family events.
10. **Cemetery Sexton Records:** Some cemeteries have detailed records kept by the sexton, which may include more information than just the gravestone inscription.
11. **Coroner's Records:** In cases of sudden or unusual deaths, coroner's records may exist and provide details about the deceased and the circumstances of their death.
12. **Institutional Records:** If an ancestor was in a hospital, orphanage, asylum, or correctional facility, records from these institutions may contain biographical information.
13. **Social Security Applications (US):** Applications for Social Security can provide birth dates and parents' names.
14. **Passenger Lists and Immigration Records:** These records often include age, place of birth, and sometimes the name of a spouse or other family members traveling together.

15. **Tax Records:** While they don't provide vital dates, tax records can help place an ancestor in a specific location at a particular time, which can help narrow down searches for other records.
16. **Mortuary Records:** Funeral homes keep records of the individuals they have handled, which may include biographical details.

When vital records are missing, the key is to think broadly about other documents that might have been created during your ancestor's lifetime or shortly after their death that would likely contain the information you seek. The information you gather from these alternative sources can often be used to piece together a compelling case for your ancestor's vital facts and relationships, even without a formal birth, marriage, or death certificate. Document all the sources you consult in your research log, including those that did not yield the desired information.

By understanding the foundational importance of vital records, knowing where to find them, and being prepared to explore alternative sources when they are unavailable, you are well-equipped to gather some of the most crucial evidence in your ancestry detective work. These records will provide the solid structure for building the detailed story of your family's past. Now, let's move on to another incredibly valuable resource: census records.

Charles Pembroke

Chapter 6: Unlocking Stories in the Census: A Snapshot of the Past

As your ancestry detective work progresses, you've begun to lay a solid foundation using vital records (births, marriages, and deaths) and the invaluable information gathered from your living relatives. Now, it's time to introduce another cornerstone of genealogical research: census records. While vital records provide crucial data points about specific life events, census records offer something unique – snapshots of your ancestors and their households at specific moments in time.

Imagine being able to peek into your ancestors' homes on a particular night, seeing who was living there, their ages, where they were born, what they did for a living, and their relationships to one another. This is the power of census records. They provide context and detail that can bring your family history to life and offer vital clues for further investigation.

This chapter will guide you through the world of census records, explaining their significance, how they evolved, where to find them, and how to extract the rich stories hidden within their columns of data.

More Than Just Names: The Rich Information in Census Records

At first glance, a census record might seem like a simple list of names and numbers. However, upon closer examination and with an understanding of the context in which they were created, census records reveal a wealth of information that goes far beyond just identifying individuals. They paint a picture of households, communities, and even national trends at specific points in time.

What kind of rich information can you expect to find in census records? The exact details vary depending on the country and the specific census year, but common elements include:

1. **Names of Household Members:** The names of everyone living in the household on the census night are recorded. This includes the head of the household, their spouse, children, other relatives, boarders, lodgers, servants, and sometimes even visitors. This immediately shows you the composition of the family unit at that moment.
2. **Relationships to the Head of Household:** The relationship of each person to the head of the household is usually specified (e.g., wife, son, daughter, mother, father, servant, boarder). This is fundamental for confirming family structures and relationships.
3. **Age:** The age of each individual is recorded. This allows you to estimate their birth year and track their age across different census years.
4. **Sex:** Male or Female.
5. **Marital Status:** (e.g., single, married, widowed, divorced).
6. **Place of Birth:** This is an incredibly valuable piece of information, indicating the town, county,

state, or country where each individual was born. This guides your research to earlier locations.
7. **Occupation:** The occupation of each adult (and sometimes older children) is recorded, providing insights into their work lives and the economy of the time.
8. **Literacy and Education:** Some census years recorded whether individuals could read or write, or if they attended school.
9. **Immigration and Citizenship Details:** Later census records, particularly in countries with significant immigration, often asked about the year of immigration, naturalization status, and country of origin.
10. **Disability and Health Information:** Some census years included questions about physical or mental disabilities.
11. **Property Ownership:** Later US censuses asked about home ownership (owned or rented) and sometimes the value of the home or farm.
12. **Language Spoken:** In some census years and locations, information about the language spoken was collected.
13. **Military Service:** Some census years included questions about military service.
14. **Enumeration District and Dwelling/Family Number:** These administrative details help locate the record and can aid in understanding the order in which the enumerator visited houses.

15. **Street Address and House Number:** In urban areas, the specific address was often recorded, allowing you to pinpoint your ancestors' homes on historical maps.

Beyond these specific data points, census records provide context. By looking at the households enumerated before and after your ancestors, you can identify their neighbors (a key element of the FAN principle). By examining the occupations in a particular area, you can understand the local economy. By observing migration patterns indicated by birthplaces, you can see how communities were formed and changed.

Census records are a treasure trove of information, offering a window into the lives of your ancestors and the times in which they lived. They are a crucial resource for extending your family tree, confirming relationships, and uncovering details about your ancestors' lives that may not be found in other records.

The Evolution of the Census: Changes in Questions and Coverage Over Time

Census taking has a long history, dating back to ancient times, primarily for taxation or military purposes. Modern, systematic censuses, designed to enumerate the entire population and collect demographic information, are a relatively recent development. Understanding how the census evolved in the country you are researching, as well as the types of questions asked in different years, is vital for utilizing these records effectively.

Here's a brief overview of the evolution of the census in the UK and the US, two of the most commonly researched countries:

United Kingdom:
- **Early Censuses (before 1841):** While some earlier enumerations and surveys exist (like the Domesday Book of 1086, which is not a census in the modern sense), the first regular decennial (every 10 years) census in Great Britain was held in 1801. However, the early censuses (1801, 1811, 1821, 1831) were primarily statistical, focusing on the number of people, their occupations, and housing. They typically did *not* list the names of all individuals in a household, which limits their genealogical value for tracing specific ancestors.
- **1841 Census (England, Wales, and Scotland):** This is the first UK census that is truly valuable for genealogists as it listed the names of *every* person in the household. It also recorded age (though often rounded down to the nearest 5 for adults), sex, occupation, and whether they were born in the same county.
- **1851 Census onwards:** Subsequent censuses (1851, 1861, 1871, 1881, 1891, 1901, 1911) progressively added more detailed questions, including:
    - Exact age and relationship to the head of household became standard.

- More detailed birthplaces (county and country).
- Information on disability.
- In later censuses, details on the number of years married, the number of children born, and the industry of employment were included.
- **1931 Census (England and Wales):** This census was destroyed by fire in 1942, a significant loss for English and Welsh genealogy.
- **1939 Register:** Created just before World War II to issue identity cards and rationing, the 1939 Register serves as a partial census substitute for England and Wales, providing names, dates of birth, occupations, and addresses. Access to information for individuals who are still living is restricted for privacy.
- **1941 Census:** No census was taken in the UK in 1941 due to the war.
- **Later Censuses:** Subsequent censuses (1951, 1961, etc.) are generally subject to a 100-year privacy rule before being released to the public for genealogical research. The 1921 census was released in early 2022.

United States:
- **First Census (1790):** The US Constitution mandates a census every 10 years. The first census in 1790 was very basic, listing only the name of the head of the household and then categorizing other household members by age and sex (free white males over 16, free white

males under 16, free white females, all other free persons, slaves). This limits its genealogical value for identifying all individuals.
- **Early Censuses (1800-1840):** These censuses continued the pattern of listing only the head of household by name and categorizing others, with some variations in the age categories over time.
- **1850 Census:** This was a pivotal year for US genealogy, as it was the first census to list the names of *every* free person in the household. It also included age, sex, color (race), birthplace, occupation, and value of real estate owned.
- **1860 Census:** Similar to 1850, with the addition of the value of personal estate.
- **1870 Census:** Included additional questions about parentage (whether parents were foreign-born) and literacy.
- **1880 Census:** A very detailed census that included relationship to the head of household, marital status, place of birth of the individual and their parents, and more detailed information about occupation and health. This is often considered one of the most valuable censuses for genealogists.
- **1890 Census:** Tragically, the majority of the 1890 US Federal Census was destroyed by fire in 1921, a significant loss for US genealogy. Surviving fragments exist for some states.
- **1900 Census:** A detailed census that included questions about immigration year, number of years in the US, and citizenship status

for foreign-born individuals, as well as the number of years married and the number of children born and living for married women.

- **1910 Census:** Similar to 1900, with some variations in questions.
- **1920 Census:** Included questions about language spoken.
- **1930 Census:** Included questions about home ownership, home value/monthly rent, and radio ownership.
- **1940 Census:** Included questions about migration, education, and employment status.
- **1950 Census:** The most recently released US census available for public research. Includes supplementary questions for some individuals.
- **Later Censuses:** Subject to a 72-year privacy rule in the US. The 1960 census will be released in 2032, and subsequent censuses will follow the same pattern.

General Trends in Census Evolution:

Across many countries, the trend in census taking has been towards:

- Listing all individuals by name.
- Collecting more detailed information about each individual and household.
- Increased standardization of questions and procedures.

Understanding these changes is crucial when you are researching a specific period and location. Knowing what questions were asked in a particular census year helps you see what information you *might* find and interpret the data accurately.

Accessing Census Records: Online Databases and Microfilm

Fortunately, for the modern ancestry detective, accessing census records is now easier than ever before, thanks to widespread digitization. The vast majority of genealogically accurate census records for countries such as the UK and the US are available online.

1. **Major Genealogy Platforms (Subscription and Free):**
    - **Ancestry:** Has extensive collections of US, UK, Canadian, Australian, and other census records with powerful search capabilities.
    - **FamilySearch:** Offers free access to a vast collection of digitized and indexed census records from around the world. Their collection of US and Canadian censuses is exceptionally comprehensive.
    - **Findmypast:** Excellent for UK and Irish census records.
    - **MyHeritage:** Has significant collections of census records, with strengths in the US, UK, and European countries.

These platforms provide both searchable indexes and the ability to view digital images of the original census schedules.

2. **National Archives Websites:** The national archives of some countries (e.g., National Archives of Ireland) provide online access to their census records, sometimes for free or with a pay-per-view model.

3. **Local Library Access:** As mentioned in Chapter 4, many public libraries offer free access to Ancestry Library Edition or other genealogy databases that include census records. This is a great way to access these resources without a personal subscription.

4. **Microfilm (Less Common Now, but Still Relevant):** Before digitization, census records were primarily accessed on microfilm in archives, libraries, and genealogical centers. While most researchers now use online access, microfilm collections may still exist. They may be relevant for less commonly digitized census years or locations, or for viewing records that are not yet available online. FamilySearch Family History Centers often have extensive microfilm collections that can be ordered for research purposes.

Tips for Accessing Census Records:

- **Start Online:** Begin your search on major online platforms, such as FamilySearch (free), and consider exploring subscription sites if needed, using free trials or library access.

- **Check Multiple Platforms:** Different platforms may have different indexes or image quality for the same census, and some collections may be exclusive to one site.
- **Understand Coverage:** Be aware of which census years and geographical areas are covered by the platform you are using.
- **Note the Source Information:** When you find a census record, carefully record the full source citation, including the census year, state/county/parish, enumeration district, sheet number, and line number.
- **Save and Organize Images:** Download or save the digitized image of the census page and organize it in your digital filing system with a clear file name.

Accessing census records online is relatively straightforward once you identify the relevant platforms. The key is to understand what's available and how to search and utilize these resources effectively.

Searching Strategies for Census Records: Name Variations, Location, and Neighbors

Finding your ancestors in census records requires effective searching strategies, especially when dealing with common names, variations in spelling, or transcription errors in indexes. Don't give up if your first search doesn't yield results.

1. **Start with What You Know:** Begin by searching for the head of the household's name, the census year, and the known location (country, state/county, town).
2. **Be Flexible with Spelling:** As discussed in Chapter 4, names were often misspelled in census records due to the enumerator's hearing, literacy, or interpretation of handwriting. Search using common variations of the surname and given name. Use wildcard characters (*, ?) if the search engine allows them.
3. **Search by Location Only (If Name Search Fails):** If you are having trouble finding an ancestor by name, and you are confident about the location where they were living in a particular census year, try browsing the census records for that specific enumeration district. Look for families with similar surnames or individuals who match the approximate ages of your ancestors.
4. **Utilize the FAN Principle (Family, Associates, Neighbors):** If you know the names of your ancestor's spouse, children, siblings, or other relatives, try searching for them in the census. You might find the entire family enumerated together. Also, look at the households enumerated immediately before and after your ancestor's household; these were their neighbors, who were often related or

came from the same place. Searching for known neighbors can sometimes help you locate your ancestor.

5. **Estimate Age Ranges:** Instead of searching for a precise age, use a range (e.g., +/- 5 years) to account for potential inaccuracies in recorded ages.
6. **Consider Abbreviations and Initials:** Sometimes, only initials or abbreviations of given names were recorded.
7. **Look for Unexpected Household Members:** Be prepared to find individuals living with your ancestors whom you didn't know about – boarders, lodgers, servants, or extended family members. These individuals can provide clues about your ancestors' lives and connections.
8. **Refine Your Search with Additional Information:** Once you get initial results, use other known information (birthplace, occupation) to filter and refine your search and confirm that the individuals you've found are indeed your ancestors.
9. **Check for Partial Records:** Be aware that some census records may be damaged, incomplete, or missing for specific areas.
10. **Use the Research Log to Track Searches:** Record every search you perform in your research log, including the search terms used and the results. This prevents you from repeating searches and helps you keep track of

what you've tried.

Effective census searching often requires a combination of flexibility, creativity, and persistence. Don't be afraid to try different search strategies and utilize the clues you have from other records and interviews.

Interpreting Census Data: Understanding Columns, Abbreviations, and Enumerator Practices

Once you find a census record that you believe includes your ancestors, the next step is to interpret the information presented carefully. Census schedules are organized into columns, each representing a specific piece of information collected by the enumerator. Understanding these columns, standard abbreviations, and the enumerators' practices is crucial for accurate interpretation and analysis.

1. **Read the Column Headings:** Before you start extracting information, carefully read the headings of each column on the census schedule. These headings clearly indicate what information was being collected in that particular column (e.g., "Name," "Relationship to head of household," "Age," "Place of Birth," "Occupation"). Be aware that column headings and their order changed between census years.

2. **Understand "Dwelling House" and "Family/Household":** Census records typically list dwellings (physical structures) and then families or households within those dwellings. Multiple families or individuals might be listed within the same dwelling.
3. **Interpret Relationships:** Pay close attention to the "Relationship to head of household" column. Understand what terms like "wife," "son," "daughter," "mother," "father," "boarder," "lodger," and "servant" meant in the context of the period.
4. **Age and Date of Birth:** Census records asked for age, which can be used to estimate a birth year. However, ages were not always recorded precisely, and people may have provided inconsistent ages across different censuses. Use the age as a guide, but try to find a birth record for a precise date. Later censuses sometimes asked for the month and year of birth.
5. **Place of Birth:** Pay close attention to the level of detail provided for birthplace (state, county, town, country). This is a key clue for researching the previous generation. Be aware that people sometimes gave inconsistent birthplaces.
6. **Occupations:** Try to understand what the listed occupations entailed during that

time. Use online resources or historical dictionaries to research unfamiliar occupational terms. The consistency of an occupation across census years can provide insights into an ancestor's work life.
7. **Abbreviations:** Enumerators often used abbreviations to save space and time. Common abbreviations include:
    1. Relationships (e.g., "W" for wife, "S" for son, "D" for daughter, "Gd" for granddaughter, "Bo" for boarder, "Lo" for lodger, "Se" for servant).
    2. Marital Status (e.g., "M" for married, "S" for single, "Wd" for widowed, "D" for divorced).
    3. Literacy (e.g., "Yes" or "No" for reading/writing).
    4. Birthplaces (e.g., state abbreviations). Familiarize yourself with common abbreviations for the census year and location you are researching.
8. **Enumerator's Practices:** Understand that census enumerators were individuals who were sometimes paid by the name or household enumerated, which could lead to rushing or inconsistencies. Their handwriting varied, and they might have made mistakes in recording information.

Some may have interpreted questions differently.

9. **Blank or Dashed Entries:** Blank entries or dashes in a column usually indicate that the question did not apply to that individual or that the enumerator did not obtain the information.
10. **Supplemental Schedules (US):** Some US censuses had supplemental schedules that collected additional information on specific populations (e.g., the "Defective, Dependent, and Delinquent Classes" schedules). These are less commonly used in basic genealogical research, but they can exist.

Careful, column-by-column interpretation of the census schedule, combined with an understanding of historical context and enumerator practices, will allow you to extract the maximum amount of information and avoid misinterpretations.

Beyond Your Direct Line: Using Census Records to Trace Extended Family

Census records are not only valuable for tracing your direct ancestors but also for uncovering information about their siblings, spouses' families, and other extended relatives. Applying the FAN principle (Family, Associates, Neighbors) is particularly effective when working with census data.

1. **Siblings of Your Direct Ancestors:** Census records are an excellent way to identify the siblings of your direct ancestors. Look at the household of your ancestor's parents; all the children living with them on the census night are likely siblings. Follow these siblings across subsequent census years to learn about their lives, spouses, and children, which can help you connect with living cousins.

2. **Spouses' Families:** Once you identify an ancestor's spouse in a marriage record or family group sheet, use census records to find the spouse living with their own parents before their marriage. This allows you to trace the spouse's family line.

3. **Children of Your Ancestors:** Census records show your ancestors' children living in the household. Follow these children across subsequent censuses as they grow up, marry, and form their own households. This is how you trace descendant lines.

4. **Relatives Living in the Same Household:** Census records often reveal extended family members living with your direct ancestors (e.g., aging parents, unmarried siblings, nieces, nephews, cousins). These individuals can provide clues about connections between different branches of your family.

5. **Neighbors:** As mentioned, look at the households enumerated immediately before and after your ancestors. Neighbors were often related or came from the same place.

Researching their families might reveal connections to your own or provide clues about migration patterns.

6. **Associates:** While not explicitly listed as "associates" in the census, you can sometimes infer connections based on shared occupations, places of origin, or religious affiliations listed in the census data for individuals in the same community.

7. **Using Birthplaces to Find Related Families:** If multiple families in the same neighborhood or town list the exact specific or unusual birthplace, it's a strong indication that they may be related or migrated together.

8. **Identifying Potential Sibling Groups:** If you find multiple young children with the same surname and similar birthplaces in a census, but no parents listed, they might be orphaned siblings living with other relatives.

9. **Tracking Families Over Time:** Follow entire family units across multiple census years to see how the household composition changes as children are born, grow up, leave home, and parents age.

Census records provide a snapshot in time, but by piecing together information from multiple census years and applying the FAN principle, you can reconstruct the lives and relationships of your extended family, adding depth and breadth to your family tree.

Charles Pembroke

Mapping Your Ancestors: Using Census Data to Understand Neighborhoods and Communities

Census records are inherently geographical. They enumerate individuals within specific locations, providing information that can help you understand the neighborhoods and communities where your ancestors lived. Combining census data with maps is a powerful technique for visualizing your ancestors' world.

1. **Identify the Enumeration District:** Every census record is part of a larger enumeration district. This district represents the specific geographical area that a single enumerator was responsible for covering. Knowing the enumeration district is crucial for locating records and understanding the local context.

2. **Find Historical Maps of the Area:** Search online or in archives for historical maps of the town, city, or county where your ancestors lived during the census year. Look for maps that show streets, property boundaries, and significant landmarks.

3. **Locate Your Ancestors' Street and House (If Listed):** If the census record includes a specific street address or house number (more common in urban areas), try to locate that address on a historical map. This allows you to see exactly where your ancestors lived with their neighbors, workplaces, and other important locations.

4. **Map the Residences of Neighbors and Relatives:** Plot the locations of your ancestors' neighbors and known relatives (identified through the FAN principle in the census) on the historical map. This can reveal patterns of settlement, migration, and community clustering.

5. **Understand Geographical Features:** Use maps to understand the geographical features of the area – rivers, hills, roads, railroads – and how they might have impacted your ancestors' lives and movements.

6. **Explore the Surrounding Area:** Once you've located your ancestors on a map, explore the surrounding area. What were the nearby businesses, churches, schools, and other institutions? This provides context for their daily lives.

7. **Analyze Migration Patterns within the Census:** By looking at the birthplaces of individuals within a community, you can see if people migrated from the same regions, indicating potential chain migration or existing kinship networks.

8. **Use Gazetteers and Atlases:** Historical gazetteers (geographical dictionaries) and atlases can provide valuable information about the characteristics of a place during a specific time.

Combining census data with historical maps allows you to move beyond abstract names and dates and visualize the physical world in which your ancestors lived. It adds a spatial dimension to your research and can reveal connections and patterns that might not be apparent from the records alone.

Identifying Clues for Further Research: Occupations, Birthplaces, and Other Hints

Every piece of information in a census record is a potential clue that can lead you to further research. As you extract data from census schedules, always be thinking about what new avenues of investigation each detail might open up.

1. **Birthplace:** The birthplace listed for each individual is a direct clue for researching the previous generation. Once you know where an ancestor was born, you can focus your search for their birth record and their parents in that specific location and period.
2. **Occupation:** An occupation can lead you to:
    - **City Directories:** These often list individuals by name and occupation, providing addresses and sometimes employer information.
    - **Professional or Trade Directories:** Specific directories existed for particular professions or trades.
    - **Union Records:** If the occupation was unionized, records might exist.

- **Business Records:** If the ancestor owned a business, records might be found in local archives or historical societies.
- **Military Records:** Certain occupations might be linked to military roles.

3. **Immigration Year and Naturalization Status:** For foreign-born ancestors, this information is crucial for finding passenger lists and naturalization records.
4. **Marital Status and Years Married:** This can help you estimate the year of marriage and focus your search for a marriage record.
5. **Names of Other Household Members:** The names of spouses, children, parents, siblings, and other relatives living in the household provide names to search for in different records (vital records, other censuses, etc.).
6. **Literacy:** Knowing if an ancestor could read or write might lead you to school records or other educational institutions.
7. **Disability or Health Information:** This information, while potentially sensitive, could lead you to institutional records or medical records if they exist and are accessible.
8. **Street Address:** Can guide searches in city directories, land records, and historical maps.
9. **Military Service (if listed):** Provides a clue to search for military records.
10. **Neighbors' Information:** As discussed, the birthplaces, occupations, and movements of neighbors can provide clues about migration

patterns and potential relationships.

As you transcribe or extract information from a census record, keep a running list of the clues you find for each individual. Record these clues in your research log and use them to plan your next steps. Each census record you see is not an endpoint, but a valuable stepping stone to uncovering more of your family's story.

Dealing with Missing or Damaged Census Records: Alternative Sources

While census records are incredibly valuable, they are not always available or complete. As we saw with the 1890 US census and the 1931 England and Wales census, entire collections can be lost. Individual pages or sections can also be damaged or missing. When you encounter a gap in the census records for your ancestors, you need to turn to alternative sources to bridge that gap.

Here are some alternative records that can help fill the void when census records are missing or damaged:

1. **Substitute Censuses or Enumerations:** Some states or localities conducted their own censuses in between the national census years. These can provide valuable information for those intervening years.
2. **Tax Records:** Tax lists often enumerated heads of households and sometimes included information about property owned, which can

help place ancestors in a specific location at a particular time.
3. **Voter Lists and Poll Books:** These records list eligible voters in a specific location and time.
4. **City Directories:** City directories list residents (typically heads of household) by name and address, and often include occupations. They were usually published annually and can help track ancestors' movements within a city.
5. **Land Records:** Deeds, mortgages, and other land records can prove an ancestor's presence in a location and may mention family relationships.
6. **Probate Records:** Wills and administrations confirm death and often name heirs, indicating family relationships.
7. **Military Records:** Draft registration cards, service records, and pension files can provide valuable information, including age, residence, and sometimes family details.
8. **Church Records:** Baptism, marriage, and burial registers can help place individuals in a specific location at a particular time and provide information about relationships.
9. **Newspaper Articles:** Local news articles, mentions in social columns, or business advertisements can indicate an ancestor's presence in a community.
10. **School Records:** Enrollment records can provide information about a child's age and parentage.

11. **Court Records:** Various court records might mention individuals and their residences.
12. **Institutional Records:** Records from hospitals, poorhouses, orphanages, or prisons may contain biographical information.
13. **Cemetery Records:** Burial records and gravestone inscriptions provide death dates and can confirm presence in a location.
14. **Passenger Lists:** For immigrant ancestors, passenger lists confirm their arrival and can provide their age and, sometimes, their intended destination.

When faced with missing census data, think about what other types of records were being created during that period and in that location that might have recorded your ancestor's presence or provided similar demographic information. Be creative in your search for alternative sources, and remember to document all your efforts in your research log.

Census Secrets and Stories: What You Can Learn About Your Ancestors' Lives

Beyond the names, dates, and numbers, census records hold the potential to reveal compelling stories and secrets about your ancestors' lives. By examining the details closely, comparing information across census years, and considering the historical context, you can gain a deeper understanding of their experiences, challenges, and triumphs.

The Ancestry Detective

1. **Household Composition and Family Dynamics:** Examine who was living in the household. Were there extended family members, boarders, or servants? This can reveal economic circumstances, family support systems, or involvement in local industries.
2. **Migration Patterns:** Trace your ancestors across census years and note changes in their place of residence and birthplaces of their children. This reveals their migration paths and can lead you to research the reasons behind their moves, such as economic opportunity, land availability, or joining family.
3. **Economic Status:** Occupations and property ownership information can provide insights into your ancestors' economic standing and social class. Compare their situation across different census years.
4. **Life Cycle Events:** Observe how the household changes over time as children are born, grow up, leave home, marry, and as parents age or pass away. Census records track the natural progression of family life.
5. **Unexpected Residents:** The presence of individuals who don't seem to fit the immediate family unit (e.g., a person with a different surname and an unclear relationship) can be a clue to investigate further. They might be relatives, boarders, or individuals in need of support.
6. **Inconsistencies and Clues to Secrets:** Note any significant inconsistencies in names, ages,

or birthplaces across different census years. While some might be simple errors, they could also hint at efforts to conceal information or navigate challenging circumstances.
7. **The Impact of Historical Events:** Observe how major historical events (like economic depressions or wars) might be reflected in your ancestors' occupations, household composition, or migration patterns.
8. **Community and Neighborhood:** By examining the occupations and birthplaces of your ancestors' neighbors, you can learn about the characteristics of their community and whether they lived among people from similar backgrounds.
9. **Tracing Women's Lives:** Census records are particularly valuable for tracing women, as they are consistently listed by name in later censuses, even if other records, such as land ownership, primarily focused on men. Tracking a woman across census years can help you identify her maiden name (by finding her in her parents' household) and the names of her children.
10. **Identifying Potential Orphans or Widows:** Households headed by women or containing young children without parents present may indicate widowhood or children living with relatives who are orphans.

By approaching census records with curiosity and a willingness to look beyond the basic facts, you can uncover fascinating stories about your ancestors' lives, their relationships, and the world they inhabited. These snapshots in time provide invaluable context and detail, making your family history a much richer and more compelling narrative. With your understanding of vital records and census records, you are now equipped to tackle other essential record types in your ancestry detective work.

Charles Pembroke

Chapter 7: Investigating Immigration and Migration: Tracing Ancestors' Movements

Your ancestry detective work thus far has focused on establishing the key events of your ancestors' lives – their births, marriages, and deaths – and placing them in households at specific points in time through census records. As you build this foundational structure, you'll inevitably begin to notice something fundamental about human history and, likely, your own family's story: people move.

Whether driven by economic necessity, political upheaval, religious freedom, or simply the promise of a new life, migration has been a constant force throughout history. Understanding and tracing your ancestors' movements, both across international borders (immigration and emigration) and within their own countries (internal migration), is crucial for piecing together their full story and breaking down genealogical brick walls. A birth record in one country followed by a marriage record in another, or a family appearing in census records in different states or counties, are clear indicators of migration, and they present a new set of challenges and opportunities for the ancestry detective.

This chapter will guide you through the process of investigating your ancestors' journeys. We will explore the motivations behind migration, the types of records that document movement, where to find these records, and how to use them to reconstruct the paths your ancestors took.

The Migratory Urge: Understanding Historical Patterns of Movement

Why did your ancestors move? Understanding the historical context of migration is vital for effective research. People didn't just randomly pick up and leave; their movements were often driven by powerful "push" and "pull" factors related to the conditions in their homeland and the opportunities (real or perceived) in their destination.

Push Factors (Reasons to Leave):
- **Economic Hardship:** A lack of employment opportunities, poverty, famine (as seen in the Great Famine in Ireland), and land scarcity have historically been major drivers of emigration.
- **Political Instability and Persecution:** War, political oppression, and lack of civil liberties have forced many to seek refuge elsewhere.
- **Religious Persecution:** Individuals and groups have migrated to escape religious discrimination or to find places where they could practice their faith freely (e.g., the Pilgrims seeking religious freedom in North America).
- **Environmental Disasters:** Natural disasters, crop failures, and environmental

degradation could make an area uninhabitable or unsustainable.
- **Social Inequality:** Lack of opportunity or rigid social structures could motivate people to seek societies with greater perceived equality.

Pull Factors (Reasons to Go To a Specific Place):
- **Economic Opportunity:** The promise of jobs, higher wages, and the chance to own land has been a powerful magnet. The availability of fertile land in North America, the industrial revolution in urban centers, and the gold rushes are examples.
- **Political Freedom and Stability:** The allure of democratic governments, the rule of law, and safety from persecution drew immigrants to certain countries.
- **Religious Tolerance:** The ability to practice one's religion without fear was a significant pull for many.
- **Established Networks:** Migrants often followed family members, friends, or neighbors who had already moved, creating chain migration patterns and providing support networks in the new location.
- **Advertising and Promotion:** Sometimes, countries or companies actively recruited immigrants to fill labor needs or settle new territories.
- **Perceived Better Quality of Life:** The general idea of a safer, healthier, or more prosperous life in a new land.

Understanding the historical events and conditions in your ancestors' homeland and potential destinations during the time they migrated can provide crucial context and help you predict where they might have gone and what records might exist. For example, if your Irish ancestors emigrated in the mid-19th century, the Great Famine was likely a significant push factor, and established Irish communities in the United States, Canada, or Australia might have influenced their destination.

Internal migration, which involves moving within a country, is also driven by similar factors, often related to seeking better economic opportunities, relocating to join family, or escaping difficult conditions in a specific region. The westward expansion in the United States, the movement from rural to urban areas during industrialization in the UK and elsewhere, and internal displacement due to conflict or disaster are examples of significant internal migration patterns.

Recognizing that migration was often a response to specific historical circumstances will help you focus your research and interpret the records you find.

Immigration Records: Passenger Lists and Border Crossings

For ancestors who crossed international borders, immigration records are among the most important sources you can find. These records document their arrival in a new country and can provide crucial details about their origin, age, and travel companions.

The Ancestry Detective

The most common types of immigration records are passenger lists and border crossing records.

1. **Passenger Lists:**
   - **What they are:** Lists of individuals traveling on a ship or other vessel, typically created at the port of departure or arrival.
   - **Information often included:**
   - Passenger's full name (sometimes with title like Mr./Mrs.).
   - Age.
   - Sex.
   - Occupation.
   - Country or place of origin/last permanent residence.
   - Port of embarkation (where they boarded the ship).
   - Port of destination (where the ship was going).
   - Name of the ship.
   - Date of arrival.
   - Sometimes, physical description or details about health.
   - Later passenger lists (early 20th century onwards) often included more detailed information, such as:
     - Marital status.
     - Literacy (can they read/write).
     - Race or ethnicity.
     - Name and address of a relative in the country of origin.

- Name and address of a relative or contact person in the country of destination.
- Final destination within the new country.
- Whether they had been to the country before.
- Who paid for their passage.
    - The amount of money they were carrying.
    - Height, eye color, hair color.
    - Place of birth.
2. **Where to find them:** Major genealogy platforms (Ancestry, FamilySearch, Findmypast, MyHeritage) have extensive collections of digitized passenger lists for various countries, particularly for arrivals in the United States, Canada, Australia, and the UK. National archives and immigration museums in destination countries often hold the original records or digitized copies on their websites.
3. **Border Crossing Records:**
4. **What they are:** Records created at land borders, particularly between the United States and Canada or Mexico.
5. **Information often included:** Similar information to passenger lists, but for individuals crossing by land, train, or ferry. May include details about previous crossings.
6. **Where to find them:** Primarily found in the national archives of the countries involved (e.g., National Archives of the United States, Library and Archives Canada). Some collections are available on major

online genealogy platforms.

Tips for Using Immigration Records:
- **Know the Approximate Arrival Date and Port:** Having an estimated date and port of arrival significantly narrows down your search. Use census records (which often asked for immigration year), family stories, or other documents to get an idea.
- **Be Flexible with Spelling:** Names could be misspelled by the ship's purser or the immigration official. Search for variations of your ancestor's name.
- **Look for Family Members:** If your ancestor traveled with family, search for other known family members on the same passenger list.
- **Note the Port of Embarkation:** This can provide a clue about the specific region or city in the country of origin your ancestor departed from.
- **Pay Attention to "Last Permanent Residence" vs. "Place of Birth":** Sometimes, the list records where they were living just before the journey, which might not be their birthplace.
- **Examine the Entire Page:** Look at the other passengers on the same page. Were they from the same village or region? Were they traveling together? This can reveal migration networks.
- **Note the Final Destination:** Later passenger lists often recorded the final

destination within the new country, guiding your research to their first place of settlement.
- **Look for Relatives in the Destination Country:** The name and address of a relative or contact person in the destination country can provide a crucial link to family or friends who sponsored or assisted their immigration.
- **Check Both Departure and Arrival Records:** While arrival records are more common online, departure records (if they exist) can sometimes provide additional information.

Finding an ancestor on an immigration record is often a breakthrough moment, providing concrete evidence of their journey and valuable clues about their origins.

Port of Entry Research: Exploring Major Ports and Their Records

Immigrants typically arrived at specific ports of entry, and these ports often have unique record collections and historical contexts that are important for the ancestry detective to understand. Focusing your research on the major ports where your ancestors likely arrived can be very effective.

Major Ports and Their Significance:
- **Ellis Island, New York, USA:** Operated from 1892 to 1954, Ellis Island was the main port of entry for millions of immigrants to the United States. The records created here are extensive and available on the free Ellis Island website

(ellisisland.org) and major genealogy platforms. The earlier main port in New York was Castle Garden (1855-1890).
- **Boston, Massachusetts, USA:** Another significant port for arrivals in the US, particularly for immigrants from Ireland and Canada.
- **Philadelphia, Pennsylvania, USA:** An important early port of entry for immigrants to the US, especially from Germany and Ireland.
- **Baltimore, Maryland, USA:** A key port for immigrants, particularly from Germany and Central Europe.
- **New Orleans, Louisiana, USA:** A major port for arrivals in the southern US, with significant immigration from Ireland, Germany, and Italy.
- **San Francisco, California, USA:** The primary port of entry on the West Coast, significant for immigrants from Asia and Latin America (Angel Island was a separate immigration station in San Francisco Bay, known for processing Asian immigrants).
- **Liverpool, England, UK:** A major transatlantic port of departure and arrival, particularly for travel to and from North America.
- **Southampton, England, UK:** Another significant port for transatlantic travel.
- **London, England, UK:** A historical port with records of arrivals from various parts of the world.
- **Quebec City and Halifax, Canada:** Major ports of entry for immigrants to Canada.

- **Melbourne and Sydney, Australia:** Key ports for arrivals in Australia.

Researching Specific Ports:

- **Utilize Port-Specific Websites and Databases:** Many major ports of entry have dedicated websites or online databases that may contain records or indexes not available elsewhere. The Ellis Island website is a prime example.
- **Understand the Immigration Process at That Port:** The procedures and record-keeping practices could vary between ports and over time. Researching the history of immigration at a specific port can help you understand the records created there.
- **Look for Records Beyond Passenger Lists:** Ports might also have records related to immigrant aid societies, detention centers, or medical inspections.
- **Explore Local Archives and Historical Societies:** Archives and historical societies in port cities may hold unique collections related to immigration and the immigrant experience in that specific location.
- **Be Aware of Changes Over Time:** Ports of entry may change, and immigration processes have evolved in response to legislation and historical events.

Focusing your research on the likely port of arrival, based on your ancestor's origin and destination, can significantly streamline your search for immigration records and provide valuable context for their arrival experience.

Naturalization Records: Becoming a Citizen

For immigrants who chose to make their new country their permanent home, the process of becoming a citizen (naturalization) often created a series of records that are incredibly valuable for genealogists. These records can provide details about their arrival, their intent to become a citizen, and biographical information.

The naturalization process and the records created varied significantly by country and over time. In the United States, for example, the process evolved through different legislative acts.

Typical Stages and Records of Naturalization (primarily US context):
1. **Declaration of Intention (First Papers):**
    - **What it is:** A statement filed by an immigrant indicating their intention to become a citizen. This could be filed shortly after arrival.
    - **Information often included:** Immigrant's name, country of origin, date and port of arrival, and renunciation of allegiance to their former country. Early records might be very brief. Later records are more detailed.

- **Genealogical Value:** Provides proof of intent to become a citizen, confirms country of origin, and gives clues about arrival.

2. **Petition for Naturalization (Second Papers):**
   - **What it is:** Filed after meeting residency requirements (which changed over time), this was a formal petition to the court to become a citizen.
   - **Information often included:** Immigrant's name, address, occupation, date and place of birth, date and port of arrival, name of spouse and children (often with their birth dates and places), and witnesses who could attest to the immigrant's residency and character.
   - **Genealogical Value:** Extremely valuable as it can provide precise birth information, arrival details, and information about the immigrant's family, including children who might not appear in other records. The witnesses are often relatives or friends, providing leads for the FAN principle.

3. **Certificate of Citizenship:**
   - **What it is:** The final document granted after the petition was approved and the oath of allegiance was taken.
   - **Information often included:** Immigrant's name and confirmation of citizenship. Usually less detailed than the

petition.

Where to Find Naturalization Records:
- **Courts:** Naturalization proceedings historically took place in various courts – federal, state, and local. Records may be held in the archives of these courts or transferred to national or state archives.
- **National Archives:** In the United States, the National Archives and Records Administration (NARA) holds extensive collections of federal naturalization records.
- **State and Local Archives:** State and local archives may hold records from state and local court naturalizations.
- **Online Databases:** Major genealogy platforms have digitized and indexed significant collections of naturalization records, particularly for the United States. FamilySearch has a growing collection.

Tips for Using Naturalization Records:
- **Check for Both Declaration and Petition:** The petition is usually more detailed, but the declaration can also provide valuable information, mainly if the petition is not found.
- **Note All Information:** Extract every piece of information from the record, including details about family members and witnesses.
- **Verify Information with Other Sources:** Information on naturalization records was provided by the immigrant, and while generally

reliable, it's always a good idea to corroborate details with other documents, such as census entries or vital records.

- **Look for Consistent Details:** Compare the arrival information provided in the naturalization record with passenger lists to ensure they match.
- **Research the Witnesses:** The witnesses listed on a petition for naturalization were often individuals who knew the immigrant well, frequently family members or close friends. Researching them can uncover connections to your ancestor.

Naturalization records are a goldmine of information for tracing immigrant ancestors, providing crucial details about their origins, arrival, and family structure in their new country.

Internal Migration: Moving Within a Country

While international immigration often involved dramatic journeys across oceans, internal migration – moving within a country's borders – was a far more common experience for many of our ancestors. Tracking these movements is just as crucial for genealogical research, as people left behind records in the places they lived.

Internal migration could involve moving between:

- **States or Provinces:** (e.g., moving from New York to Ohio in the US, or from Wales to England in the UK).
- **Counties:** Moving between adjacent or distant counties.
- **Towns or Cities:** Moving from rural areas to urban centers, or between different towns.
- **Neighborhoods:** Moving within the same city.

Why Trace Internal Migration?
- **Locating Records:** Many records are organized by location. Knowing where and when your ancestor lived in a specific place is essential for finding census records, land records, tax records, court records, and local vital records.
- **Understanding Family History:** Internal migration often reflects economic opportunities, family connections (moving to be near relatives), or other personal circumstances.
- **Breaking Down Brick Walls:** If you lose track of an ancestor in one location, tracing their potential migration paths is crucial for finding them in a new place.

Clues to Internal Migration:
- **Census Records:** The birthplace listed for individuals and their children, and changes in residence between census years, are key indicators of internal migration.

- **Vital Records:** Birthplaces listed on marriage or death certificates for individuals born elsewhere.
- **City Directories:** Tracking individuals moving between addresses within a city or appearing in directories in different cities over time.
- **Land Records:** Buying and selling land in different locations.
- **Tax Records:** Appearing on tax lists in different places.
- **Court Records:** Legal proceedings in different jurisdictions.
- **Newspaper Articles:** Mentions of individuals moving to or from a town.
- **Family Letters and Diaries:** Discussions of moves or plans to move.
- **Oral Family History:** Stories about the family moving from one place to another.

Tracing internal migration requires piecing together clues from various record types across different locations.

Sources for Tracking Internal Migration: Deeds, Tax Records, and Local Histories

When tracing internal migration, you will rely heavily on records that document an individual's presence in a specific location at a particular time. Beyond census and vital records, several other sources are beneficial for tracking internal movements.

1. **Land and Property Records (Deeds, Mortgages):** Buying and selling land creates a clear record of presence in a specific location. Deeds can sometimes mention the previous residence of the buyer or the new residence of the seller, providing direct evidence of migration. Tracking an ancestor's land transactions across different counties or states is a powerful way to trace their movements. These records are typically found in county courthouses or their archives and are increasingly being digitized.
2. **Tax Records:** Tax lists were created annually or biannually to record individuals liable for various taxes (poll tax, property tax). Appearing on a tax list in a specific location is strong evidence of residence there. Tracking an ancestor's appearance (or disappearance) from tax lists in different counties can help pinpoint their movements. These records are often found in county courthouses or state archives.
3. **City Directories:** Published annually in many towns and cities, city directories list residents (usually heads of household) with their addresses and occupations. They are invaluable for tracing individuals who move within a town or appear in different city directories over time. Many historical city directories have been digitized and are available on major genealogy platforms or library websites.

4. **Voter Lists and Poll Books:** These records enumerate eligible voters in a specific precinct or town. Appearance on a voter list typically indicates residence and, in many cases, citizenship.
5. **Court Records:** Records of lawsuits, criminal proceedings, or probate matters can place individuals in a specific jurisdiction at a particular time.
6. **Newspapers:** Local newspapers often contained news about residents moving to or from the area, social visits, or business activities that can indicate the presence in a location.
7. **Church Records:** Joining or leaving a church in a new location can indicate a move. Church records may mention previous residences.
8. **School Records:** Enrollment records for children can indicate the family's residence.
9. **Account Books and Business Records:** If an ancestor was involved in a business, their name might appear in account books or other business records that indicate their location.
10. **Local Histories and Gazetteers:** These published resources offer historical context on settlement patterns, migration routes, and the development of specific areas. Gazetteers can help you identify smaller localities mentioned in records.

Tracing internal migration often requires a combination of these record types, piecing together fragmented evidence from different sources and locations to reconstruct your ancestor's movements.

Understanding Push and Pull Factors: Why Did Your Ancestors Move?

Revisiting the concept of push and pull factors (discussed at the beginning of this chapter) is crucial *after* you have found evidence of your ancestors' migration. Once you know *when* and *where* they moved, you can research the historical conditions in their origin and destination locations during that given period to understand *why* they might have moved.

- **Research the History of the Origin Location:** What were the economic conditions, social issues, political climate, or environmental factors in the place your ancestors left during the years leading up to their departure? Was there a famine, economic depression, land shortage, or political unrest?
- **Research the History of the Destination Location:** What opportunities or conditions existed in the place your ancestors moved to during the time of their arrival? Was there available land, job growth in specific industries, or an established community of people from their homeland?
- **Consider Personal Circumstances:** Beyond the broad historical factors, consider your ancestors' circumstances. Were they seeking to join family members who had already

migrated? Were they recently married and looking to establish their household? Were they escaping a personal difficulty or seeking a fresh start?

By understanding the push and pull factors at play, you gain a deeper appreciation for the challenges and motivations behind your ancestors' migration decisions. This adds a layer of human context to the factual data you collect from records. It transforms a simple change of address into a narrative of aspiration, resilience, or necessity.

Mapping Migration Routes: Visualizing Your Ancestors' Journeys

Visualizing your ancestors' migration journeys on maps can be incredibly helpful for understanding their movements, identifying potential research areas, and presenting your findings to others.

1. **Use Online Mapping Tools:** Online tools like Google Maps or historical mapping websites can help you locate the towns, counties, and regions where your ancestors lived and trace the routes they might have taken between these locations.

2. **Create a Migration Timeline:** Develop a timeline that lists the dates and locations where you have found your ancestors in records. This timeline can be overlaid onto a map to visualize their movements over time.

3. **Utilize Historical Maps:** Historical maps can show old roads, canals, railways, and geographical features that your ancestors would have used during their journeys. They can also reveal the development of towns and cities over time.

4. **Plot Birthplaces on Maps:** If a census record lists the birthplaces of children born in different locations, plot these birthplaces on a map to visualize the family's movement between census years.

5. **Map the Origins of Immigrant Groups:** If you are researching immigrant ancestors, use maps to explore the regions in their homeland from which people were emigrating and the areas in the destination country where they were settling.

6. **Consider Modes of Transportation:** Think about how your ancestors would have traveled during their migration (walking, horse-drawn carriage, train, ship, canal boat). The available modes of transportation would have influenced the routes they took.

Mapping your ancestors' migration routes transforms abstract geographical data into a tangible representation of their journeys, making their experiences more real and understandable.

Case Studies in Migration: Following Families Across Continents and Countries

Examining real-life examples of tracing families across continents and countries can illustrate the process and the types of records used in this process. While a full case study is beyond the scope of this overview, consider these simplified examples:

- **The Irish Family to America:** A family is found in Irish Griffith's Valuation records (a property survey from the mid-19th century) in a specific county. They disappear from later Irish records. A search of US passenger lists for major ports like New York or Boston around the time of the Great Famine reveals a family with the same surname and similar ages arriving. Subsequent US census records then track the family's movement from the port city to an inland county, and then across several states as they seek land and opportunity. Vital records in the US confirm marriages and births of children born in the new country, and eventually, a death record might verify their place of birth in Ireland, corroborating the passenger list information.
- **Internal Migration in the UK:** A family is found in the 1841 UK census in a rural English village, with the father working as an agricultural laborer. By the 1851 census, they appear in a growing industrial town in a different county, with the father and older sons working in a factory. Subsequent censuses track their lives in the

industrial town. Marriage records for the children list their residence in the town at the time of marriage, and death records confirm their passing there. Land records might show them renting a small house in the town. This pattern reflects the migration from rural areas to industrial centers during the Victorian era.

These case studies emphasize the value of utilizing a combination of records, including census, vital records, immigration records, and land records, from both the origin and destination locations to reconstruct the migration story. Persistence and a willingness to search in multiple places are key.

The Impact of Migration on Family: How Moving Shaped Your Ancestors' Lives

Beyond the factual details of when and where your ancestors moved, it's essential to consider the profound impact that migration had on their lives and the lives of their families. Moving to a new place, whether across an ocean or a few counties away, was a significant undertaking that brought both opportunities and challenges.

Consider the impact of migration on:
- **Family Structure:** Did the whole family move together, or did individuals migrate first and send for others later (chain migration)? How did migration affect the extended family left behind?

- **Economic Circumstances:** Did migration lead to improved economic opportunities, or were there periods of hardship and struggle in the new location?
- **Social Adaptation:** How did your ancestors adapt to a new culture, language, and social environment? Did they settle in communities with others from their homeland?
- **Cultural Preservation and Change:** Did they maintain their cultural traditions and language, or did they assimilate into the new culture?
- **Challenges and Hardships:** What were the difficulties they faced during their journey and in settling in a new place (e.g., poverty, discrimination, illness, separation from family)?
- **Opportunities and Successes:** What were the positive outcomes of their migration? Did they find better jobs, acquire land, or provide greater opportunities for their children?
- **Identity:** How did migration shape their sense of identity and belonging? Did they still identify with their homeland, or did they adopt a new national or regional identity?

By reflecting on these questions and looking for clues in the records and family stories, you can gain a deeper understanding of the human experience of migration and how these journeys shaped not only your ancestors' lives but also the trajectory of your family history. Tracing migration is not just about following a line on a map; it's about understanding the courage, resilience, and sacrifices of those who came before you. With your growing knowledge of vital records, census records, and the intricacies of migration, you are well on your way to becoming a skilled ancestry detective, ready to tackle other important record types.

Charles Pembroke

Chapter 8: Discovering Military Records: Finding Information in Service Records

As your ancestry detective work continues, piecing together the lives of your ancestors through vital records, census data, and migration patterns, you may encounter individuals who served in the military. Military service, whether in times of conflict or peace, often generated records that can provide a wealth of genealogical information, offering insights into your ancestors' lives, experiences, and sometimes, their families, that you might not find anywhere else.

Beyond the historical significance of their service, military records can contain crucial details, such as age, birthplace, physical description, occupation, and even information about spouses, children, or parents, particularly in pension or enlistment records. For ancestors who are difficult to trace through other means, military records can sometimes provide the breakthrough needed to extend your family tree.

This chapter will guide you through the process of discovering and utilizing military records in your genealogical research. We will explore the types of records available, where to find them, how to interpret their unique terminology, and how they can help you unlock more stories about your ancestors' lives.

Charles Pembroke

Beyond the Battlefield: The Value of Military Records for Genealogists

When we think of military records, our minds might immediately go to battle histories and unit movements. While these are certainly part of the picture, military records created to document the service of individual soldiers, sailors, airmen, and marines contain a surprising amount of personal and genealogical information.

Why are military records so valuable for the ancestry detective?

1. **Proof of Service and Presence:** Military records confirm that an individual served in a particular military force during a specific time, placing them in a specific location (or series of locations) when they may be challenging to locate in other records.
2. **Biographical Details:** Enlistment or service records often include valuable biographical information provided at the time of entry into service. This can include:
    - Full name (and sometimes aliases).
    - Age or date of birth.
    - Place of birth.
    - Occupation before service.
    - Physical description (height, weight, hair color, eye color, complexion, distinguishing marks like scars or tattoos). This is unique information not typically found in other records.

- Marital status.
- Nearest relative or next of kin (sometimes including their address and relationship).

3. **Tracing Movements:** Service records can detail the units an individual served with, the locations where those units were stationed, and dates of transfers, deployments, or movements. This helps you track your ancestor's geographical movements during their period of service.
4. **Details of Service:** Records document enlistment and discharge dates, rank, promotions, training, disciplinary actions, injuries, and medical treatment. While not strictly genealogical, this information provides insight into your ancestor's experiences during their service.
5. **Pension and Bounty Land Records (Especially Valuable):** For soldiers who served in specific conflicts, particularly in the United States, pension applications (filed due to disability or by widows/dependents after death) and bounty land applications (grants of land for military service) can be wealthy sources of genealogical information. These often required proof of identity, marriage, and the legitimacy of children, leading to the inclusion of marriage certificates, family Bible records, affidavits from relatives and neighbors, and detailed personal testimonies. These records can sometimes connect multiple generations and branches of a family.
6. **Identifying Relatives:** Pension records, in particular, frequently name spouses, children,

and sometimes even parents or siblings who provided supporting testimony for a claim. Enlistment records may also name a next of kin.
7. **Understanding Causes of Death or Disability:** Military medical records or pension files can provide detailed information about injuries, illnesses, and the causes of death related to service.
8. **Connecting with Historical Events:** Military records place your ancestors directly within the context of major historical conflicts and events, providing a deeper understanding of their experiences and the times in which they lived.
9. **Filling Gaps in Other Records:** If you are missing vital records or census entries for a period when an ancestor was in the military, their service records may provide alternative documentation of their age, birthplace, and whereabouts.
10. **Finding Burial Locations:** Military burial records can confirm a veteran's death and provide details about their burial location in a military cemetery or other designated burial site.

Military records offer a unique window into a significant period of an ancestor's life and can provide invaluable genealogical clues, particularly within pension and bounty land files. Don't overlook the possibility of military service in your family history research.

Identifying Military Ancestors: Starting with Family Stories and Basic Records

Before you start searching for military records, you need to identify which of your ancestors might have served. This often begins with the clues you've already gathered from your initial research.

1. **Family Stories and Oral History:** Your living relatives are the first and best source for identifying potential military ancestors. Ask about family members who served, the conflicts they were in, their branch of service, and any stories or memorabilia related to their military experience. Even vague mentions, such as "Grandpa was in the war," can serve as a starting point.

2. **Vital Records:** Death certificates may indicate if a person was a veteran. Marriage records or birth certificates might list an occupation as "soldier," "sailor," etc.

3. **Census Records:** Later census records (particularly in the US, starting from 1840 onwards, with more detailed questions in later years) often included questions about military service, including the conflict in which the individual served or whether the individual was a veteran or an army widow. Look for specific columns related to military service.

4. **Obituaries and Cemetery Records:** Obituaries often mention military service. Gravestones in military cemeteries or even

civilian cemeteries may indicate military service through the use of symbols or inscriptions. Cemetery burial records may also note veteran status.

5. **Pension Records (for Widows or Dependents):** If a female ancestor is listed in census records as a military widow or is receiving a pension, this is a strong indication that her deceased husband served.

6. **Published County or Local Histories:** These histories sometimes include lists of residents who served in various conflicts.

7. **Military Discharge Papers (if found among family documents):** Finding physical discharge papers among family heirlooms is a direct confirmation of service.

8. **Fraternal Organization Records:** Some fraternal organizations, such as the Grand Army of the Republic in the US for Civil War veterans, maintained records of their members, often including details of their military service.

9. **City Directories:** In some periods, city directories indicated veteran status or listed veterans' organizations.

Once you have a potential military ancestor in mind, with an approximate period and location, you can begin to focus your search for specific military records.

The Ancestry Detective

Exploring Different Conflicts and Service Periods: Records by Era and Branch

Military record availability and content vary significantly depending on the conflict, the country, and the branch of service (e.g., Army, Navy, Marines, Air Force). Understanding the major conflicts your ancestors might have participated in and the types of records generated during those periods is essential for effective searching.

United Kingdom Military Records (Examples):
- **British Army:** Records exist for various periods, including:
  - **Pre-18th Century:** Records are scarce and often found in collections related to specific regiments or events.
  - **18th and 19th Centuries (e.g., Napoleonic Wars, Crimean War, Boer War):** Records like muster rolls, pay lists, and pension records exist. Records become more standardized over time.
  - **World War I (1914-1918):** Extensive service records exist for soldiers who enlisted in the British Army. Tragically, many World War I service records were destroyed by bombing during World War II, known as the "Burnt Documents." However, surviving "Unburnt Documents" and pension records, held separately, are invaluable. Medal rolls are also crucial for identifying service.

- **World War II (1939-1945):** Service records from World War II are generally still held by the Ministry of Defence and are subject to access restrictions due to privacy. You can typically request records of deceased service personnel with proof of death and relationship.
- **Royal Navy:** Records exist for various periods, including muster rolls, pay books, and service records.
- **Royal Air Force (formed 1918):** Records exist for officers and airmen from its formation onwards.
- **Other Forces:** Records also exist for the Royal Marines, auxiliary forces, and colonial forces.

United States Military Records (Examples):
- **Colonial and Revolutionary War:** Records are fragmented and can be found in state archives, historical societies, and collections related to specific units or events. Pension and bounty land records from the Revolutionary War are particularly valuable and often contain details provided to prove service and eligibility.
- **War of 1812:** Service and pension records exist.
- **Mexican-American War:** Service and pension records exist.
- **Civil War (1861-1865):** Records for both Union and Confederate soldiers are extensive.

- **Union:** Service records (compiled from various original documents), pension records (very detailed and valuable for genealogical information), draft records.
- **Confederate:** Service records (though many were lost or destroyed), some limited pension records (available from individual Southern states).

- **Spanish-American War:** Service and pension records exist.
- **World War I (1917-1918):** Draft registration cards (for men aged 18-45) are a valuable resource, providing age, birth date, physical description, and nearest relative. Service records also exist.
- **World War II (1941-1945):** Extensive service records exist for all branches. However, a significant portion of Army and Air Force personnel records from 1912-1960 were destroyed in a fire at the National Personnel Records Center in St. Louis in 1973 (known as the "NPRC fire"). Despite the loss, many records survived or can be reconstructed from auxiliary records. Draft records also exist for this period.
- **Korean War, Vietnam War, and later conflicts:** Records are generally held by the National Archives and are subject to access restrictions due to privacy.

General Considerations by Branch of Service:

- **Army:** Records often include details about regiments, companies, and land-based movements.
- **Navy/Marines:** Records focus on ships, deployments, and service at sea or in coastal areas.
- **Air Force (or earlier Air Corps/Royal Flying Corps):** Records detail squadrons, airfields, and flight-related activities.

Understanding the specific record types generated for the conflict and branch of service relevant to your ancestor is crucial for knowing what to look for and where to find it. Genealogy websites and archival guides often provide overviews of the available military records for different periods and services.

Accessing Military Records: National Archives, Online Databases, and Veterans' Organizations

Various institutions, primarily national archives, hold military records, but many have also been digitized and made available on online genealogy platforms.

1. **National Archives:**
    - **The National Archives (UK) at Kew, London:** Holds a vast collection of British military records, including Army, Navy, and Air Force service records, medal rolls, and pension records. Many collections have been digitized and are available through their own website

(often with a pay-per-view model) or on partner genealogy platforms.

- **National Archives and Records Administration (NARA) in the United States:** NARA holds federal military records. Personnel files for soldiers discharged after certain dates are held at the National Personnel Records Center (NPRC) in St. Louis. Older records are held at the main NARA facility in Washington, D.C., and regional archives. You can request records from NARA, though there can be fees and waiting times.
- **National Archives in Other Countries:** If your ancestor served in the military of another country, research their national archives to find out about their military record holdings and access procedures.

2. **Online Databases:**
   - **Major Genealogy Platforms (Ancestry, FamilySearch, Findmypast, MyHeritage):** These sites have digitized and indexed significant collections of military records from various countries and conflicts. Ancestry has particularly strong collections of US military records. Findmypast is excellent for British military records. FamilySearch has a growing collection of digitized military records, many of which are available for free.
   - **Specific Military Genealogy Websites:** Some websites specialize in military records for specific conflicts or countries.

- **Fold3 (fold3.com):** A subscription website owned by Ancestry that specializes in military records, offering a wide range of digitized collections, significant for US military history.
- **Forces War Records (forces-war-records.co.uk):** A subscription website focused on British military records.

3. **Veterans' Organizations:** Historical veterans' organizations, such as the Grand Army of the Republic in the US and the British Legion in the UK, often maintained records of their members. Their archives or historical collections might hold valuable information.

4. **State Archives (US):** Some US state archives hold records of state militia units or soldiers who served from that state.

5. **County and Local Archives:** Local archives might hold records related to local military units or veterans' groups.

6. **Regimental and Unit Archives:** Some historical military regiments or units maintain archives or museums that hold valuable records.

Tips for Accessing Military Records:

- **Start with What You Know:** Use the clues you have (name, approximate service dates, conflict, branch) to narrow down your search.
- **Search Online Databases First:** Begin your search on the major online platforms that cover the relevant country and time period.
- **Be Flexible with Search Terms:** Try variations of names and locations.

- **Utilize Indexes:** Online indexes can help you find potential records, but always try to view the original document image.
- **Be Patient with Physical Record Requests:** Requesting records from national archives can take time and involve fees.
- **Be Aware of Privacy Restrictions:** Records of recently deceased service personnel may have access restrictions.
- **Check for Records of Both Sides (in Civil Wars):** If researching a civil war (like the US Civil War), remember to search for records for both sides of the conflict.
- **Explore Related Record Sets:** If you find a service record, look for associated pension records, medal rolls, or unit histories.
- **Document Everything:** Record all your searches and findings in your research log, including details about the source of the military record.

Accessing military records can sometimes be challenging due to the volume of records, historical losses, and access restrictions. However, with patience and a systematic approach, you can often find valuable information about your ancestors' military service.

Interpreting Military Documents: Understanding Terminology and Forms

Military records often contain specialized terminology, abbreviations, and forms that can be confusing to those unfamiliar with them. Understanding these elements is crucial for accurately interpreting the information you find.

1. **Understand the Purpose of the Document:** What kind of record is it? (e.g., enlistment paper, muster roll, service record, pension application). The purpose of the document will dictate the type of information it is intended to collect.
2. **Familiarize Yourself with Military Ranks and Units:** Learn the different ranks (e.g., Private, Sergeant, Lieutenant, Captain, Colonel) and the organizational structure of military units (e.g., Company, Regiment, Battalion, Brigade, Division – or their equivalents in Navy/Air Force like ship names, squadrons).
3. **Decipher Abbreviations:** Military records, especially older ones, often use numerous abbreviations for ranks, units, locations, and actions. Look for online guides or dictionaries of military abbreviations for the relevant time period and country.
4. **Understand Military Terminology:** Be prepared to encounter terms related to military life, training, battles, and medical conditions that may be unfamiliar. Use online resources or historical dictionaries to look up unfamiliar terms.
5. **Examine All Parts of the Form:** Military forms can be standardized, but often have sections for various details. Carefully examine every box and entry on the form.

6. **Pay Attention to Dates:** Note enlistment dates, discharge dates, dates of transfers, and dates of battles or deployments.
7. **Look for Details of Physical Description:** This unique information can help you confirm that the record belongs to your ancestor.
8. **Note the "Remarks" or "Notes" Sections:** These sections can sometimes contain valuable narrative information about an individual's service, conduct, or specific events.
9. **Understand Medical Terminology:** Pension records, in particular, may contain detailed medical information related to injuries or illnesses sustained during service. Medical terminology from past centuries can differ significantly from that used today.
10. **Be Aware of Different Forms for Different Periods:** The specific forms used to record military service changed over time. Familiarize yourself with the forms relevant to your ancestor's service period.

Interpreting military documents requires patience and a willingness to learn new terminology. Utilize online resources and guides to help you decipher the information and understand the context of your ancestor's military experience.

Pension Records: A Wealth of Family Information

For ancestors who served in specific conflicts, particularly in the United States, pension records are arguably the most genealogically valuable type of military records. These records were created when veterans, or their widows or dependents, applied for financial assistance based on their service. The application process often required extensive documentation of identity, service, disability (for veteran pensions), and family relationships (for widow or dependent pensions).

Why US Pension Records are So Valuable:

- **Proof of Marriage:** Widow's pension applications required proof of a legal marriage to the veteran. This often involved submitting marriage certificates, copies of marriage register entries, or affidavits from witnesses to the marriage.
- **Identification of Children:** Widow's pension applications required listing all minor children of the veteran, including their birth dates and places. This is an invaluable source for identifying children who might be missed in census records or for whom birth records haven't been found.
- **Affidavits from Relatives and Neighbors:** To support their claims, applicants often submitted affidavits (sworn statements) from relatives, friends, and neighbors who could

attest to the veteran's identity, service, marriage, or the legitimacy of children. These affidavits can name siblings, parents, cousins, and neighbors, providing crucial links to other individuals and families.

- **Veteran's Testimony:** Veteran's pension applications often include the veteran's detailed testimony about their service, injuries, illnesses, and personal life. This can provide rich biographical detail and insights into their experiences.
- **Medical Information:** Pension files contain detailed medical records related to service-connected disabilities, including doctors' reports and examinations.
- **Proof of Death:** Widow's pension applications required proof of the veteran's death, often including death certificates or testimony from witnesses.
- **Prior Marriages:** Pension files might contain information about previous marriages of the veteran or the applicant.

Finding US Pension Records:

- **National Archives and Records Administration (NARA):** holds the original federal pension application files for most U.S. conflicts. You can request copies of these files from NARA.
- **Online Databases:** Fold3 (subscription) and Ancestry (subscription) have digitized significant collections of US pension records,

particularly for the Revolutionary War and the Civil War. FamilySearch also has some indexed pension records available for free.

UK Pension Records: While not as consistently detailed as US Civil War pensions, British military pension records (held at The National Archives and sometimes available online) can also contain valuable information about service, injuries, and sometimes family details.

Pension records can be lengthy and complex, containing dozens or even hundreds of pages of documents. However, the genealogical riches they can contain make the effort of finding and interpreting them well worthwhile. They are often the key to unlocking information about family relationships and personal experiences that are not recorded anywhere else.

Draft Records and Enrollment Lists: Identifying Potential Service

Even if an ancestor did not serve in the military, they may appear in records related to military conscription or enrollment. These records can still provide valuable genealogical information and indicate potential military service or eligibility.

1. **Draft Registration Cards (US):**
    - **World War I and World War II:** Millions of American men were required to register for the draft during these conflicts, regardless of whether they were eventually called to serve.

- **Information Included:** Draft cards typically include the individual's name, address, date and place of birth, age, race, occupation, employer, nearest relative or contact person (often a parent, spouse, or sibling), and a physical description.
- **Genealogical Value:** Provides a specific birth date and place, confirms residence at the time of registration, gives an occupation, and crucially, names a nearest relative, which can help confirm family connections.
- **Where to Find Them:** Digitized collections of World War I and World War II draft registration cards are widely available on major online genealogy platforms (Ancestry, FamilySearch, Fold3, MyHeritage).

2. **Militia and Enrollment Lists:** In earlier periods, men of a certain age were often required to enroll in local militias. Lists of these enrollments can exist in local or state archives. While they may not indicate active service, they place an individual in a specific location at a particular time and indicate their eligibility for military duty.

3. **Conscription Records:** Records related to conscription or impressment (forcing individuals into military service, particularly in the Navy in earlier periods) can also exist.

Tips for Using Draft Records and Enrollment Lists:

- **Use Them to Estimate Birth Dates and Places:** Draft cards provide specific birth dates and places, which are valuable even if the ancestor didn't serve.
- **Confirm Residence:** Appearance on a draft list or enrollment list confirms your ancestor's residence in a specific location at the time the list was created.
- **Note the Nearest Relative:** The name of the nearest relative on a draft card can provide a direct link to a parent, spouse, or sibling.
- **Look for Physical Description:** This unique information can help confirm identity and provide interesting details.
- **Consider it a Clue for Further Research:** If an ancestor appears on a draft list but you don't find military service records, it might indicate they were not called up or their records were lost. However, their service eligibility is noted.

Draft records and enrollment lists are valuable supplementary resources that can provide genealogical information and indicate potential military connections, even for ancestors who did not see active combat.

Records of Military Units: Tracing Your Ancestor's Company or Ship

Once you have identified that an ancestor served in a particular military force during a specific conflict, researching the history of their military unit (regiment, company, ship, squadron) can provide valuable context for their service and sometimes reveal additional information about the individuals within that unit.

1. **Identify the Unit:** Service records or pension files typically name the specific unit(s) your ancestor served with. Note the full name and number of the regiment, company, ship, or squadron.
2. **Research the Unit's History:** Look for published histories of the unit, online resources dedicated to that unit, or information in archival collections. Unit histories often detail the unit's movements, battles in which it participated, and sometimes include lists of officers and soldiers.
3. **Muster Rolls and Pay Lists:** These records, often found in national archives or digitized on genealogy platforms, list the soldiers or sailors who were part of a unit at specific points in time. They can confirm your ancestor's presence in the unit and sometimes provide details about their pay or status.
4. **After Action Reports and Diaries:** Records created by unit commanders detailing their activities can sometimes mention individual soldiers for notable actions.

5. **Unit Rosters:** Lists of individuals who served in a particular unit.
6. **Regimental and Ship Logs:** For Navy or maritime service, ship logs document daily activities, locations, and significant events.
7. **Unit Associations:** Historical associations of veterans from specific units may have their archives or publications.

Genealogical Value of Unit Records:
- **Confirming Service:** Unit records can corroborate an ancestor's service in a specific unit during a particular time.
- **Placing Ancestors in Specific Locations:** Unit movements and deployments documented in unit histories or records place your ancestor in those locations.
- **Identifying Comrades:** Muster rolls and rosters list other individuals in the same unit, providing potential individuals to research for the FAN principle or to find affidavits in pension files.
- **Understanding Experiences:** Researching the battles or campaigns the unit participated in provides context for your ancestor's potential experiences during their service.

Researching your ancestor's military unit adds depth to their service history and can sometimes reveal additional genealogical clues about the individuals they served alongside.

Military Cemeteries and Burial Records: Locating Final Resting Places

For veterans, military cemeteries are often their final resting place. Records related to military cemeteries and burials can confirm a veteran's death, provide burial details, and sometimes offer additional biographical information.

1. **National Military Cemeteries:** Many countries have national cemeteries specifically for veterans. Records for burials in these cemeteries are typically held by the government agency responsible for veterans' affairs. In the United States, the National Cemetery Administration (part of the Department of Veterans Affairs) maintains a searchable online database of burials in national cemeteries.

2. **State and Local Military Cemeteries:** Some states or localities also have cemeteries dedicated to veterans.

3. **Cemetery Records:** Even if a veteran is buried in a civilian cemetery, cemetery records (discussed in Chapter 5) may indicate their military service.

4. **Online Databases (Find a Grave, BillionGraves):** These websites include millions of cemetery records and gravestone photos, often including information about military service.

5. **Military Burial Registers:** Specific registers may have been kept for military burials

during conflicts or in specific locations.

Information Found in Military Burial Records:
- Veteran's full name.
- Date of death.
- Date of burial.
- Cemetery name and location.
- Section and grave number.
- Branch of service and rank.
- Conflict served in.
- Sometimes, date and place of birth, or next of kin.

Tips for Using Military Burial Records:
- **Confirm Death and Burial Location:** These records definitively confirm an ancestor's death and burial location.
- **Verify Military Service:** The presence of an ancestor in a military cemetery or a notation of military service in civilian cemetery records confirms their service.
- **Look for Nearby Burials:** Family members were sometimes buried in adjacent plots in military or civilian cemeteries.
- **Utilize Online Cemetery Databases:** Websites like Find a Grave and BillionGraves are easily searchable and often include photos of gravestones, providing visual confirmation of inscriptions.

Military cemetery and burial records provide a final piece of the puzzle in tracing a veteran's life and can offer valuable genealogical information about their service and final resting place.

Connecting with Military History: Understanding the Context of Your Ancestor's Service

To truly understand your military ancestor's experiences, it's essential to place their service within its historical context. Researching the conflict they participated in, the specific campaigns or battles their unit was involved in, and the general conditions of military life during that era will add depth and meaning to the factual details you find in records.

1. **Research the Conflict:** Learn about the causes and major events of the war or conflict your ancestor served in. Understand the political and social climate of the time.

2. **Research the Unit's Activities:** Explore the history of your ancestor's specific regiment, company, ship, or squadron. Where were they stationed? What battles or campaigns did they participate in? What were their experiences?

3. **Understand Military Life During That Period:** Research what life was like for soldiers, sailors, or airmen during that specific era. What was the training like? What were the living conditions, food, and medical care? What were the risks and challenges they faced?

4. **Read Firsthand Accounts:** Look for diaries, letters, or memoirs written by other soldiers or sailors who served in the same

conflict or unit. These personal accounts can provide powerful insights into the daily realities of military life.

    5. **Visit Museums and Historical Sites:** Visiting military museums or historical battlefields can provide a tangible connection to your ancestor's experiences.

    6. **Utilize Online Resources and Books:** Numerous websites, books, and documentaries are dedicated to military history and the experiences of service personnel in different conflicts.

By connecting with the military history relevant to your ancestor's service, you move beyond just collecting names and dates and begin to understand the challenges, sacrifices, and experiences that shaped their time in the military. This adds a rich layer of human story to your genealogical research and honors their service in a meaningful way. Military records, when examined within their historical context, offer a powerful means of uncovering the courage and experiences of your ancestors.

Chapter 9: Unlocking Land and Property Records: Using Deeds and Other Land Documents

As your ancestry detective work moves beyond the foundational records of births, marriages, deaths, and censuses, you will begin to explore other record types that can fill in the details of your ancestors' lives. Among the most valuable, and sometimes most challenging, of these are land and property records. While primarily created to document ownership and transfer of land, these records often contain a wealth of genealogical information that can help you confirm relationships, trace migration patterns, identify neighbors, and understand your ancestors' economic standing.

Unlike vital records or census data, which enumerate individuals at specific points in time, land records document transactions over time, often spanning decades or even centuries. They provide a continuous link to one particular place and the individuals who owned or occupied the land there. For ancestors who seem to disappear from census records or whose relationships are unclear, land records can sometimes provide the crucial evidence needed to piece together their story.

This chapter will guide you through the world of land and property records, explaining their genealogical value, the different types of records you may encounter, where to find them, how to interpret their unique language, and how to use them to unlock more secrets about your family's past.

Beyond Ownership: How Land Records Reveal Family Connections and Movements

It might seem counterintuitive that documents primarily concerned with real estate transactions could be so crucial for tracing people. However, in historical contexts, land ownership was often deeply intertwined with family structure, economic stability, and social standing. Land was a primary form of wealth and was frequently passed down through generations, bought and sold within families or communities, and used to secure loans or provide for dependents.

Why are land and property records valuable beyond simply proving who owned a piece of land?

1. **Confirming Relationships:** Deeds often mention the relationships between the parties involved in a transaction (e.g., "John Smith to his son, Thomas Smith," or a wife relinquishing her dower rights). These explicit statements of relationship are invaluable for confirming family connections when other records are missing or ambiguous.
2. **Tracing Migration Patterns:** The buying and selling of land in different locations provides concrete evidence of your ancestors' movements. A deed might state that the grantor (seller) is "of County X" but is selling land in County Y, indicating a potential move. Similarly, a

grantee (buyer) might be listed as "of County Z" purchasing land in a new area. Tracking these transactions across different counties or states can help you reconstruct migration paths.

3. **Identifying Neighbors and Associates (FAN Principle):** Land records often describe property boundaries by referencing the land of adjacent landowners. By identifying these neighbors, you can apply the FAN principle, researching these individuals to see if they were related to your ancestors or migrated from the same place. Witnesses to deeds were also often relatives or close associates.

4. **Pinpointing Residence at a Specific Time:** Owning or transacting land in a particular location is strong evidence that your ancestor resided there at the time of the transaction, even if census records for that year are missing.

5. **Understanding Economic Status:** The amount of land owned, its value, and the nature of the transactions can provide insights into your ancestor's economic standing and prosperity.

6. **Dower and Marital Status:** In historical common law systems (including the UK and US), a wife often had a right of dower in her husband's land, meaning she had a claim to a portion of it after his death. When a married man sold land, his wife was often required to sign the deed to relinquish her dower rights. This "dower release" is crucial evidence that the man was married at the time of the sale and provides his wife's name

(often including her maiden name if mentioned in the acknowledgment).
7. **Identifying Heirs:** When an individual died, their land was often divided among their heirs according to a will or the laws of inheritance. Probate records (Chapter 10) often work in conjunction with land records to document this transfer of ownership among family members.
8. **Clues to Previous Residence or Origin:** As mentioned under migration, deeds can sometimes state the previous residence of a party, providing a direct clue to where they lived before.
9. **Understanding Property Division and Family Relationships:** Analyzing how land was divided among children or other heirs can reveal family structures and relationships.
10. **Context for Local History:** Land records are a fundamental source for understanding the historical development of a specific locality, including settlement patterns, land use, and the formation of communities.

Land records require careful reading and interpretation, but the genealogical information they can reveal makes them an invaluable resource for tracing your ancestors and understanding their lives beyond just names and dates.

Types of Land Records: Deeds, Mortgages, Grants, and Patents

The term "land records" encompasses a variety of documents created to document the ownership, transfer, and encumbrance of real property. While the specific terminology and types of records can vary by country and time period, some common types include:

1. **Deeds:**
   - **What they are:** Legal documents that transfer ownership of land from one party (the "grantor" or seller) to another (the "grantee" or buyer).
   - **Genealogical Value:** The most common and often most genealogically valuable type of land record. Contains the names of the grantor(s) and the grantee(s), a legal description of the property, the date of the transaction, the amount paid, and crucially, often mentions spouses and their dower rights, and sometimes relationships between parties. Witnesses' names are also included.
   - **Types of Deeds:** Various types of deeds exist (e.g., warranty deed, quitclaim deed), each with slightly different legal implications, but all document a transfer of ownership.
2. **Mortgages:**
   - **What they are:** Legal documents that use land as collateral for a loan. The landowner (mortgagor) grants the lender (mortgagee) an interest in the land as security for the debt. Once

the loan is repaid, a "release of mortgage" is recorded.

- **Genealogical Value:** Indicates an ancestor owned land and was involved in financial transactions. It can help place an ancestor in a specific location at a particular time. Mortgage records often name the spouse, as they may have had to sign to relinquish their dower rights.

3. **Land Grants and Patents (primarily US):**
    - **What they are:** The first transfer of land from the government (federal or state) to private ownership. A "land grant" is the legislative authorization for the transfer, and a "land patent" is the official document confirming the transfer of title.
    - **Genealogical Value:** Documents the initial settlement of land and identifies the first private owner. Can indicate military service (bounty land grants), participation in settlement programs, and provide the earliest documented link of an ancestor to a specific piece of land. Application files for land patents (like Homestead records) can be particularly rich in biographical information.

4. **Tax Records:**
    - **What they are:** Records of property assessments and taxes paid on land.
    - **Genealogical Value:** While not transferring ownership, tax records prove an individual owned property (or sometimes just resided) in a specific location in a given year.

Tracking an ancestor in tax lists over time and across different locations is a powerful way to trace their movements and confirm their presence. Tax records may also list the amount of land owned or its assessed value, providing economic context.

5. **Township Plats and Surveys (primarily US):**
   - **What they are:** Maps and records created during the survey of public lands, particularly in the rectangular survey system used in much of the western and midwestern United States.
   - **Genealogical Value:** These records document the initial division of land and can sometimes include the names of early settlers who claimed specific parcels.

6. **Manorial Records (UK):**
   - **What they are:** Records of manorial courts in England and Wales, which dealt with landholding within a manor. These can include court rolls that document the transfer of copyhold land, a type of land tenure.
   - **Genealogical Value:** For ancestors who were copyholders, these records document their relationship to the land and can sometimes include details about family members involved in inheritance or transfer. These are less common among the general population over time as freehold ownership has become more prevalent.

7. **Land Valuation Records (e.g., Griffith's Valuation in Ireland):**
   - **What they are:** Surveys and valuations of land and property for taxation purposes.

- **Genealogical Value:** Provide a snapshot of who occupied land in a specific location at a particular time, often listing both the landlord and the occupier. Griffith's Valuation (c. 1847-1864) is a crucial record for Irish genealogy, listing heads of households who occupied land or property.

Understanding the different types of land records that exist in the periods and locations your ancestors lived is the first step to utilizing them in your research.

Accessing Land Records: County Courthouses and Online Resources

Accessing land records can be a bit different from accessing vital records or census data. While an increasing number of records are being digitized, many land records still primarily reside in local government offices.

1. **County Courthouses (primarily US):** In the United States, land records are typically recorded and maintained at the county level, usually by the Register of Deeds, County Clerk, or a similar office. To access original land records, you will often need to visit the county courthouse in the county where the land was located.
   - **In-Person Research:** Visiting the courthouse allows you to search the indexes and view the original deed books. Be prepared for variations in organization

and indexing methods across different counties.
- **Requesting Copies:** You can usually request copies of specific deeds or other land documents from the county office, typically for a fee.

2. **National and State Archives (US):** The National Archives hold records related to federal land grants and patents, such as Homestead records. State archives may have documents related to state land grants or copies of county-level records.
3. **Online Databases:** The availability of digitized land records online is increasing, but the level of access varies significantly by location.
4. **Major Genealogy Platforms:** Some major platforms, such as Ancestry and FamilySearch, have digitized collections of land records for specific counties or states; however, their coverage is not as comprehensive as that of census or vital records.
5. **County Government Websites:** Some progressive county governments are digitizing their land records and making them available online, often through searchable databases.
6. **Subscription Land Record Websites:** Specialized subscription websites exist that focus specifically on digitizing and providing access to land records for various areas.
7. **FamilySearch:** FamilySearch is actively digitizing land records from county courthouses

across the United States and making them available for free on their website, often as browsable images without an initial name index.

8. **UK Land Records:**
9. **The National Archives (UK):** Holds central government land records, including records of land held by the Crown and some historical land surveys.
10. **County Record Offices:** Hold records related to land ownership within the county, including deposited manorial records, estate papers, and enclosure records.
11. **The Land Registry:** The official body responsible for maintaining a register of land ownership in England and Wales. More recent records are held here, but historical records are less likely to be in the Land Registry's purview.
12. **Online Resources:** Some digitized UK land records are available on major genealogy platforms or through specific archival websites. Manorial records are increasingly being cataloged and digitized.

Tips for Accessing Land Records:
- **Identify the Specific Location:** You need to know the county (or equivalent) where the land was located.
- **Determine the Relevant Period:** Land records are recorded sequentially, so knowing the approximate date of a transaction is helpful.
- **Check Online Resources First:** Start by searching online databases on major platforms

or FamilySearch to see if the land records for your target location and time have been digitized.

- **Visit the County Courthouse or Local Archive:** If records are not online, plan a visit or inquire about their procedures for requesting copies by mail.
- **Utilize Online Catalogs and Finding Aids:** Check the websites of county courthouses and archives for online catalogs or finding aids that describe their land record holdings.
- **Be Aware of Different Indexing Systems:** Understand how land records are indexed (often by grantor and grantee) to search them effectively.

Accessing land records often requires more targeted research based on location, but the information they can reveal about your ancestors' presence and activities in a specific place is invaluable.

Understanding Legal Descriptions: Metes and Bounds, Township and Range

Land records, particularly deeds and grants, contain legal descriptions of the property being transferred. Understanding how land was surveyed and described in the relevant period and location is essential for accurately interpreting these records. The two most common systems you will encounter in the United States are Metes and Bounds and the Public Land Survey System (Township and Range). The UK has different methods of describing property, often relying on existing boundaries and landmarks.

United States Land Description Systems:
1. **Metes and Bounds:**
    - **What it is:** An older system of describing land boundaries by using physical landmarks, directions, and distances. Descriptions follow the perimeter of the property.
    - **Examples:** "Beginning at an oak tree on the north bank of the Jones River, thence running north 45 degrees East for 100 poles to a stone marker, thence running South 30 degrees East for 80 poles to a large rock, thence running along the bank of the Jones River to the point of beginning."
    - **Where Found:** Primarily used in the original thirteen colonies and parts of states derived from them (e.g., Kentucky, Tennessee). Also used for some later land grants.
    - **Genealogical Value:** Mentions of physical landmarks (trees, rocks, rivers) can help pinpoint the location on historical maps. References to adjacent landowners (e.g., "thence running along the line of John Smith's land") are valuable for identifying neighbors.
2. **Public Land Survey System (PLSS) or Township and Range:**
    - **What it is:** A standardized system of surveying public lands into a grid of

townships (6 miles square) and sections (1 mile square). Townships are located based on principal meridians and baselines.

- **Description Format:** Land is described by referring to its location within a section, township, and range (e.g., "The Southeast Quarter of Section 16, Township 3 North, Range 5 East of the 5th Principal Meridian").
- **Where Found:** Used for surveying public lands after the Revolutionary War, encompassing most of the United States west of the original thirteen colonies (except for Texas and parts of some other states).
- **Genealogical Value:** Provides a precise geographical location for the land. Once you understand the system, you can pinpoint the exact parcel on a map. Records related to the initial survey can sometimes mention early settlers.

United Kingdom Land Description:

- **Reliance on Existing Boundaries:** Land in the UK was typically described by referencing existing features, landmarks, or the land of adjacent owners. Descriptions might be less precise in terms of measured distances and angles compared to Metes and Bounds or PLSS.
- **Place Names and Field Names:** Descriptions often refer to local place names, field names, or natural features.

- **Acreage:** The size of the parcel is usually given in acres, roods, and perches.

Interpreting Legal Descriptions:

- **Use Online Resources:** Numerous websites and guides explain the Metes and Bounds and Township and Range systems. Use online calculators or mapping tools designed for these systems.
- **Consult Gazetteers and Maps:** Use historical gazetteers to identify place names mentioned in descriptions. Use historical maps to locate landmarks and visualize the property boundaries.
- **Look for Adjacent Landowners:** Pay close attention to mentions of neighboring landowners in Metes and Bounds descriptions, as these are clues for applying the FAN principle.
- **Understand Historical Units of Measurement:** Be aware of older units of measurement used in land records (e.g., rods, perches, chains).

Understanding the legal descriptions in land records is essential for accurately locating the property your ancestors owned and interpreting the documents effectively. It requires a bit of technical knowledge, but it is a crucial skill for working with these records.

Grantor and Grantee Indexes: Navigating Land Records Effectively

Land records in courthouses and archives are typically organized chronologically within large deed books. To find a specific deed, you need to use the indexes created to help researchers locate records. The most common types of indexes are grantor and grantee indexes.

1. **Grantor Index:**
   - **How it works:** This index is organized alphabetically by the surname of the *grantor* (the person selling or giving the land).
   - **How to use it:** If you know your ancestor *sold* land, you would look them up in the grantor index for the relevant county and period. The index entry will typically include the grantor's name, the grantee's name, the date of the deed, the type of deed, and the book and page number where the original deed is recorded.
2. **Grantee Index:**
   - **How it works:** This index is organized alphabetically by the surname of the *grantee* (the person buying or receiving the land).
   - **How to use it:** If you know your ancestor *bought* or *received* land, you would look them up in the grantee index for the relevant county and time. The index entry will typically include the grantee's name, the grantor's name, the date of the deed, the type of deed, and the book and page number where the original deed is

recorded.

Using the Indexes:
- **Search Both Indexes:** To find all transactions involving your ancestor, you need to search both the grantor and grantee indexes for the time period during which they were likely involved in land transactions in that county.
- **Estimate Time Periods:** Use census records, tax records, and other documents to estimate the years your ancestor was likely living in a particular county and might have been buying or selling land.
- **Be Flexible with Spelling and Initials:** Search for variations of your ancestor's name and consider that only initials might be used in the index.
- **Note All Relevant Entries:** When you find an entry for your ancestor in an index, carefully note all the details provided, especially the book and page number, which you will need to locate the original deed.
- **Be Aware of Different Index Types:** Some older indexes may be organized differently (e.g., by the first letter of the surname or only covering specific periods). Read the introductory pages of the index to understand its organization.
- **Online Indexes:** Many digitized land record collections online have searchable indexes, which function similarly to physical indexes.

Mastering the use of grantor and grantee indexes is essential for efficiently navigating land records and locating the specific deeds relevant to your ancestors.

Deeds as Genealogical Goldmines: Identifying Relationships, Neighbors, and Migration Clues

While the primary purpose of a deed is to transfer property, the careful language and standard clauses used in historical deeds can reveal a surprising amount of genealogical information. Treat every deed involving your ancestor as a potential genealogical goldmine, examining every detail closely.

1. **Identifying Relationships:** Look for explicit statements of relationship between the grantor and grantee (e.g., "for the love and affection I have for my son"). While not all deeds between relatives explicitly state the relationship (they might be structured as a standard sale), when they do, it's a clear piece of evidence.

2. **Spouse's Name and Dower Release:** Pay close attention to mentions of the grantor's spouse and the relinquishment of dower rights. This provides the spouse's name and confirms the grantor was married at the time of the sale. The wife's acknowledgment (a separate statement often included with the deed) sometimes mentions her maiden name.

3. **Witnesses:** Witnesses to a deed were often family members, friends, or neighbors. Their names can provide clues for applying the FAN principle and identifying potential relatives or associates. Researching the witnesses' records can sometimes lead you back to your ancestor.

4. **Adjacent Landowners:** As discussed under legal descriptions, the names of adjacent landowners mentioned in Metes and Bounds descriptions are invaluable for identifying neighbors and potentially related families. Create a plat map (a map showing property boundaries and owners) of the area where your ancestor owned land, using the deed descriptions to draw the boundaries and label the neighbors.

5. **Migration Clues:** Look for statements in the deed indicating the residence of the grantor or grantee. If an individual is selling land in one county but is stated to be "of County X," it's a strong indication they have moved. Similarly, if a grantee is "of County Z" purchasing land in a new area, it documents their arrival.

6. **Previous Ownership History (Chain of Title):** A deed often references the previous owner and the deed by which the grantor acquired the property. Tracing the "chain of title" back through previous deeds can sometimes lead you to earlier ancestors who owned the land or provide clues about how the land was passed down.

7. **Mentions of Heirs:** In some cases, a deed might mention the heirs of a deceased previous owner as the grantors, providing evidence of inheritance and family relationships.

8. **Specific Clauses and Conditions:** Occasionally, a deed might include specific clauses or conditions that provide unique details

about the family or the transaction (e.g., a condition related to supporting an aging parent, or a clause about shared access to a resource).

Reading deeds requires patience and attention to detail. Don't just skim for names; read the entire document carefully, looking for all the standard clauses and any unique information that might be included. Every word can be a potential clue.

Tax Records: Tracking Ancestors Through Property Assessments

While not documenting ownership transfer, tax records, particularly property tax records, are a valuable resource for tracking your ancestors' presence in a specific location over time and understanding their economic standing.

    1. **Proof of Residence:** Appearing on a tax list in a particular county or town is strong evidence that your ancestor resided there in the year the tax was assessed.

    2. **Tracking Movements:** By examining tax lists for a specific county over several years, you can track when an ancestor first appeared on the list (indicating their arrival) and when they disappeared (indicating a potential move or death). Comparing tax lists across different counties can help you trace their migration.

    3. **Identifying Property Ownership:** Tax records typically list individuals who owned property and often describe the type and amount

of property taxed (e.g., acres of land, number of horses, value of personal property).

4. **Understanding Economic Status:** The amount of tax paid and the assessed value of property can provide insight into your ancestor's wealth and economic standing.

5. **Identifying Neighbors:** Tax lists are often organized geographically (by district or ward), and looking at the names listed before and after your ancestor can help identify their neighbors.

6. **Estimating Age (Sometimes):** Poll tax lists, which taxed adult males, can sometimes provide an estimate of an individual's age based on the age range subject to the tax.

7. **Substitute for Missing Records:** In periods or locations where census records are missing, tax records can sometimes serve as a partial substitute for placing individuals in a specific place at a particular time.

Accessing Tax Records:

- **County Courthouses and Archives:** Tax records were typically created at the county or local level and are often held in county courthouses or their archives.
- **State Archives:** State archives may hold copies of county tax lists or statewide tax records.
- **Online Databases:** Some digitized collections of tax records are available on major genealogy platforms or through state and local archival websites. FamilySearch has a growing

collection of digitized tax records.

Tax records can be tedious to search, especially if they are not indexed. Still, they provide a consistent, year-by-year record of individuals in a community and are invaluable for tracking movements and understanding economic circumstances.

Probate and Land: Connecting Estate Settlements with Property Division

Probate records (which we will explore in more detail in Chapter 10) are created after a person's death to settle their estate, including the distribution of their property. There is a strong connection between probate records and land records, as land was often a significant asset to be distributed among heirs.

    1. **Wills and Land Devise:** If an ancestor left a will, it would often specify how their land was to be divided among their heirs (spouse, children, other relatives). The will provides direct evidence of family relationships and the intended distribution of property.

    2. **Intestacy and Land Division:** If an individual died without a will (intestate), the court would oversee the distribution of their estate, including land, according to the laws of inheritance. Court records related to the administration of an intestate estate often document the division of land among the legal heirs, providing proof of relationships.

3. **Probate Inventories and Appraisals:** These documents, part of the probate file, list the deceased's assets, which would include land owned. The value of the land would be appraised.

4. **Guardianship Records and Land:** If minor children inherited land, guardianship records (also often found in probate or court records) would document who was appointed to manage the children's inheritance, including their land.

5. **Deeds Executed by Heirs:** After land was distributed through probate, the heirs might subsequently sell their inherited shares. Deeds for these sales would typically mention that the grantors are heirs of the deceased former owner, providing further proof of relationship.

When researching an ancestor who owned land, always look for their probate records. The probate file can explain how their land was distributed and provide crucial details about their family relationships that might not be found in the land records alone. Similarly, if you find a deed where the grantors are identified as heirs of a deceased individual, look for the probate records of that deceased person.

The Ancestry Detective

Mapping Your Ancestors' Land: Visualizing Their Holdings and Their Neighbors

As discussed under legal descriptions, combining land record information with maps is a powerful way to visualize your ancestors' lives and their place in a community. Creating a plat map based on deed descriptions is a key technique.

1. **Gather Deed Descriptions:** Collect the legal descriptions from all the deeds where your ancestor bought or sold land in a specific area.
2. **Obtain a Base Map:** Use a modern or historical map of the relevant county or township as your base. Section maps (in areas using the Public Land Survey System, or PLSS) are handy.
3. **Plot the Boundaries:** Using the legal descriptions (Metes and Bounds or Township and Range) and understanding the survey system, plot the boundaries of your ancestor's land on the base map. This can be done manually or using online mapping tools designed for plotting land descriptions.
4. **Identify Adjacent Landowners:** Label the names of the adjacent landowners mentioned in the deed descriptions on your map. This visually highlights your ancestor's neighbors.
5. **Add Other Relevant Locations:** Mark the locations of churches, schools, cemeteries, waterways, roads, and other significant

landmarks in the area that would have been part of your ancestor's community.

6. **Trace Changes Over Time:** Create separate maps or layers for different periods to visualize how your ancestor's landholdings changed over their lifetime or how the ownership of surrounding parcels evolved.

7. **Use Online Mapping Tools:** Websites like Google Earth or specialized genealogical mapping tools can help you visualize historical land ownership on modern satellite imagery.

Creating a map of your ancestors' land helps you move beyond abstract legal descriptions and see their property within its geographical and community context. It makes the information from land records more tangible and can reveal patterns of settlement and neighborly connections.

Case Studies in Land Research: Solving Genealogical Puzzles with Property Records

Examining real-life examples of how land records have been used to solve genealogical puzzles can illustrate their power and versatility.

- **Confirming Parentage Through a Deed:** A researcher is trying to prove that John Smith is the son of Thomas Smith. They find a deed where Thomas Smith grants a parcel of land to "my beloved son, John Smith," explicitly stating the relationship and providing clear proof that might be missing from vital records.

- **Tracing Migration with Land Transactions:** A family disappears from census records in County A. A search of land records in a neighboring county, County B, reveals a deed where John Jones of County A purchases land in County B shortly after they disappear from the first county's census. Subsequent records then find the family living in County B, confirming their migration.
- **Identifying a Wife's Maiden Name:** A researcher finds a deed where William Brown sells land, and the deed includes a dower release signed by "Sarah, wife of William Brown." The acknowledgment section states, "Sarah, wife of William Brown, being examined separately and apart from her husband, doth relinquish her right of dower in the within described premises." In an earlier deed where Sarah's father sold land, a similar dower release by a daughter named Sarah and her husband William Brown is found, and the acknowledgment in *that* deed states, "Sarah Brown, formerly Sarah White, wife of William Brown..." revealing Sarah's maiden name as White.
- **Using Adjacent Landowners to Find Relatives:** A researcher finds a deed for their ancestor, John Davis, which describes the property as bordering the land of Thomas Evans and William Williams. Researching Thomas

Evans and William Williams in census records and vital records reveals that they are John Davis's brothers-in-law, married to his sisters. This confirms the sibling relationships and provides new avenues for research.

These case studies demonstrate how carefully examining the details within land records, utilizing indexes effectively, and combining land information with other record types can provide crucial evidence for confirming relationships, tracing movements, and breaking down genealogical brick walls. Land records are not just legal documents; they are historical records that hold valuable clues about your ancestors' lives and connections. With patience and a systematic approach, you can unlock their secrets.

Chapter 10: Exploring Probate and Court Records: Wills, Administrations, and Legal Proceedings

As your ancestry detective work progresses, you've learned to utilize vital records to establish key life events, census records to glimpse households at specific times, migration records to trace movements, military records to uncover service details, and land records to track property ownership and sometimes reveal family connections. Now, we turn to another category of records that can be incredibly rich in genealogical detail: probate and court records.

While the term "probate" often brings to mind just a will, a probate file can contain a variety of documents created when a person's estate was settled after their death. These records, along with other types of court documents generated by legal proceedings, can provide direct evidence of family relationships, reveal details about your ancestors' property and possessions, shed light on family disputes, and place individuals in specific locations at particular times. For ancestors who left behind property or had legal entanglements, probate and court records can be a genealogical goldmine.

This chapter will guide you through the world of probate and court records, explaining their genealogical value, the different types of records you may encounter, where to find them, how to interpret their unique legal language, and how they can help you unlock more secrets about your family's past.

Beyond the Will: The Genealogical Riches in Probate Files

While finding an ancestor's will is often the primary goal when exploring probate records, the probate "file" or "packet" typically contains a collection of documents created throughout the entire process of settling an estate. These accompanying documents can be just as, if not more, genealogically valuable than the will itself.

What kind of genealogical riches can be found within a probate file, beyond just the will?

1. **The Will (if one exists):** This is the most direct statement of the deceased's wishes for the distribution of their property. Genealogically, wills are invaluable for:
    - **Naming Heirs:** Wills explicitly name the individuals who are inheriting property (heirs, beneficiaries, legatees). These are often spouses, children, grandchildren, siblings, or other relatives.
    - **Stating Relationships:** Wills frequently state the relationship of the heir to the deceased (e.g., "to my beloved wife, Mary," "to my son, John," "to my granddaughter, Sarah"). These are direct proofs of familial connections.

- **Identifying Property:** Wills describe the land, possessions, and money being distributed.
- **Naming Executors:** The individuals appointed to carry out the terms of the will were often family members or trusted associates.

2. **Petitions for Probate/Administration:** These initial documents filed with the court request that the will be proven (probate) or that an administrator be appointed to settle the estate if there is no will (administration). They typically name the deceased, the date of death, and the name of the person applying for probate or administration, often stating their relationship to the deceased. These petitions can be particularly useful for identifying a surviving spouse or the closest living relatives.

3. **Letters Testamentary (for estates with a will) or Letters of Administration (for intestate estates):** These official court documents authorize the executor or administrator to act on behalf of the estate. They confirm who is responsible for settling the estate and reinforce the connection to the deceased.

4. **Inventories:** These detailed lists enumerate all the personal property owned by the deceased at the time of their death.
   - **Genealogical Value:** Inventories provide a fascinating glimpse into your ancestors' daily lives and economic status. They list household goods, tools, livestock,

crops, clothing, books, and other possessions. This helps you understand their lifestyle and what was important to them. Appraisers, who valued the property, were often neighbors or associates, providing leads for the FAN principle.

5. **Appraisals:** Documents listing the estimated value of the property listed in the inventory.
    - **Genealogical Value:** Provides further insight into the deceased's wealth.

6. **Accounts:** Detailed records of the income and expenses of the estate during the probate process.
    - **Genealogical Value:** Accounts can list debts owed by or to the deceased, payments made to individuals (including potentially family members for services rendered or debts owed), and expenses related to the funeral, debts, and court fees. Payments to heirs or guardians are also recorded here.

7. **Sales Records:** If property was sold as part of the estate settlement, these records list the items sold, the purchasers, and the amounts paid.
    - **Genealogical Value:** Purchasers were often family members or neighbors, providing clues about who was in the community and who might be related.

8. **Receipts:** Receipts for payments made by or to the estate.

- **Genealogical Value:** Can name individuals involved in transactions with the estate, potentially including family members or local tradespeople.
9. **Petitions and Orders Related to Land Division:** If the deceased owned land, especially in cases of intestacy, there may be court petitions and orders related to the division of the land among the heirs. These documents explicitly name the heirs and how the land was divided, providing clear proof of relationships.
10. **Guardianship Records (often part of or linked to probate):** If minor children inherited property, the probate file might include documents related to the appointment of a guardian to manage their inheritance. Guardians were often relatives, providing further clues about family connections.

A comprehensive probate file can be a treasure trove of genealogical information, providing not only direct proof of relationships but also rich details about your ancestors' lives, possessions, and the community they lived in. Always try to find the entire probate packet, not just the will.

Wills: Identifying Heirs and Family Relationships

The will is the cornerstone of many probate files and is often the first document genealogists seek. While not everyone left a will, those who did provide a direct statement of their intentions for the distribution of their estate and, crucially, identified their beneficiaries and their relationships.

Genealogical Information in a Will:
- **Testator's Name and Residence:** The name of the person making the will and where they resided at the time. This confirms their presence in a specific location.
- **Bequests and Devises:** The will details specific gifts of personal property ("bequests") and real property (land, "devises").
- **Names of Beneficiaries/Heirs:** The individuals who are receiving property. These are the key names you are looking for.
- **Stated Relationships:** Wills frequently state the relationship of the beneficiary to the testator (e.g., "to my beloved wife," "to my eldest son," "to my daughter's children," "to my brother"). These are primary sources for proving familial connections.
- **Names of Executors:** The individuals appointed to manage the estate. These were often family members or close associates.
- **Names of Witnesses:** Individuals who witnessed the signing of the will. Witnesses were sometimes family members or neighbors.
- **Date the Will Was Written:** The date the will was created.
- **Date the Will Was Proven/Probated:** The date the court accepted the will as valid. This indicates the approximate time of death (usually shortly before the probate date).

Tips for Using Wills:
- **Read the Entire Will Carefully:** Don't just scan for names. Read the entire document to understand the testator's intentions, the property being distributed, and any conditions or instructions included.
- **Note All Names and Relationships:** Record every name mentioned in the will and the stated relationship to the testator.
- **Pay Attention to Bequests to Married Daughters:** Wills often refer to married daughters by their married names but may also mention their husbands. This can help identify a daughter's spouse.
- **Look for Bequests to Grandchildren or Other Relatives:** Wills can extend beyond the immediate family to include grandchildren, siblings, nieces, nephews, or other relatives, providing clues about broader family connections.
- **Consider What *Isn't* in the Will:** If a known child or spouse is *not* mentioned in the will, there might be a reason. They could have predeceased the testator, received their inheritance earlier, or been intentionally excluded. Further research is needed to gain a deeper understanding of the circumstances.
- **Identify Executors and Witnesses:** Research the executors and witnesses; they may be related to the testator.
- **Note the Date the Will Was Written and Probated:** The date the will was written can indicate that individuals mentioned later in the will

were still living on that date. The probate date provides an approximate death date.
- **Be Aware of Legal Terminology:** Wills use specific legal language. Consult a glossary of historical legal terms if needed.
- **Look for Mentions of Land:** Wills often describe the land being devised. Compare these descriptions with land records.

Wills are powerful documents for confirming family relationships and understanding how property was distributed among heirs. They provide a direct voice from your ancestor about their family structure and intentions.

Administrations: When Someone Died Without a Will

Not everyone left a will. When a person dies without a valid will (intestate), the court would appoint an administrator to settle their estate according to the laws of inheritance. The records created during this process, known as "administrations," can be just as genealogically valuable as a probate file with a will.

Genealogical Information in Administration Records:

- **Petition for Administration:** The initial document filed with the court requesting that an administrator be appointed. This petition is typically filed by the closest living relative(s) or a major creditor. Usually, it names the deceased, the date of death, and the name and relationship

of the person requesting administration. This is a key document for identifying surviving family members.
- **Letters of Administration:** The official court document appointing the administrator and authorizing them to act on behalf of the estate.
- **Bonds:** The administrator was typically required to post a bond as a guarantee that they would faithfully carry out their duties. Relatives or associates often served as sureties on these bonds, providing further clues about connections.
- **Inventories and Appraisals:** Similar to probate with a will, an inventory and appraisal of the deceased's personal property would be created.
- **Accounts:** Detailed records of the administrator's handling of the estate's finances. These accounts can show payments made to or received from individuals, including heirs.
- **Petitions and Orders for Distribution:** In intestate estates, the court would oversee the distribution of assets, including land, among the legal heirs according to the laws of inheritance. Court petitions and orders related to distribution explicitly name the heirs and their respective shares, providing clear evidence of relationships established by legal statutes. This is particularly valuable for identifying all surviving children when a will is absent.

- **Guardianship Records:** If minor children inherited property, records related to the appointment of a guardian would be created.

Why Administration Records Are Valuable:
While you won't find the personal bequests of a will in an administration file, the court-supervised process of settling an intestate estate creates records that are equally, if not more, valuable for identifying all legal heirs and proving familial relationships based on the laws of the time. Always look for administration records if you don't find a will for an ancestor who likely owned property or had a significant estate.

Probate Inventories and Accounts: Glimpses into Ancestors' Possessions and Lives

Beyond the legal transfer of property, the inventories and accounts within a probate file offer a unique window into your ancestors' daily lives and economic circumstances. These documents list their possessions and detail the financial transactions related to their estate.

Genealogical Value of Inventories:
- **Insights into Lifestyle and Wealth:** The items listed in an inventory reveal a great deal about your ancestors' standard of living, their occupation, their hobbies, and what they valued. Listing farming equipment, household goods,

clothing, books, tools, or even livestock paints a picture of their daily life.
- **Indications of Occupation:** The presence of specific tools or equipment can confirm or provide clues about an ancestor's occupation.
- **Identifying Family Heirlooms:** Sometimes, specific items are listed that might have been family heirlooms.
- **Appraisers as Potential Relatives or Neighbors:** The individuals appointed to appraise the estate's property were often neighbors or associates, providing leads for the FAN principle.

Genealogical Value of Accounts:
- **Confirming Debts and Creditors:** The Accounts list who the deceased owed money to or who owed money to the deceased. These individuals could be family members or business associates.
- **Funeral Expenses:** Details about funeral expenses can provide insights into social customs and costs of the time.
- **Payments to Heirs or Guardians:** Accounts document payments made to the heirs or guardians for the support of minor children, confirming who received distributions from the estate.
- **Payments for Services Related to the Estate:** Payments to individuals for services like legal work, appraising, or handling the funeral

can also be listed.

Tips for Using Inventories and Accounts:
- **Read the Entire Document:** Don't just scan for specific items. Read through the entire inventory and account to get a complete picture of the estate.
- **Research Unfamiliar Items or Terms:** You may encounter archaic terms for household goods, tools, or currency. Use historical dictionaries or online resources to understand what they were.
- **Note Names of Appraisers, Buyers (in sales records), and Individuals Mentioned in Accounts:** These individuals could be family members or neighbors.
- **Compare Inventories Over Time:** If you can find inventories for multiple generations of a family, you can see how their possessions and wealth changed over time.
- **Look for Clues About Family Relationships:** While inventories don't typically state relationships, the presence of specific items or debts owed between individuals might suggest a familial connection.

Probate inventories and accounts provide a level of detail about your ancestors' material lives and financial affairs that is often not found in other records. They help bring your ancestors to life by showing you the world they inhabited and the things they owned.

Guardianships: Records of Minor Children

When a parent died, leaving behind minor children (typically under the age of 21, though this varied historically and by location), and those children inherited property or needed care, the court would often appoint a guardian. Records related to these guardianships are frequently found within probate files or in separate court records and are invaluable for tracing minor children and identifying their relatives.

Genealogical Information in Guardianship Records:

- **Names of Minor Children:** Guardianship records explicitly name the minor children for whom a guardian is being appointed.
- **Names of Deceased Parent(s):** The records will state the name(s) of the deceased parent(s).
- **Name of the Guardian:** The individual appointed as guardian.
- **Relationship of the Guardian to the Children:** Often, the guardian was a surviving parent, a grandparent, an aunt or uncle, or another relative. The record may state this relationship, providing direct proof of familial connections.
- **Details about the Children's Property:** Guardianship records often detail the property inherited by the minor children, including land.

- **Accounts of the Guardian:** The guardian was typically required to file accounts with the court detailing how they were managing the children's inheritance and expenses. These accounts might include payments for the children's maintenance, education, or other needs.
- **Bonds:** The guardian was often required to post a bond, and the sureties on the bond were frequently relatives or associates of the family.
- **Petitions for Guardianship:** Documents filed to request the appointment of a guardian, often naming the petitioner and their relationship to the children.

Why Guardianship Records Are Valuable:
- **Identifying Minor Children:** These records serve as a primary source for identifying minor children who may be difficult to trace in other documents, especially if they died young or were not consistently listed by name in early census records.
- **Confirming Parentage:** Guardianship records explicitly link minor children to their deceased parent(s).
- **Identifying Relatives as Guardians and Sureties:** The individuals appointed as guardians or who served as sureties on guardianship bonds were often family members, providing clues about extended family connections.

- **Insights into the Lives of Minor Children:** Guardianship accounts can provide valuable details about the upbringing and expenses associated with the care of minor children.

If you find evidence in probate records or other sources that an ancestor died, leaving behind minor children, always look for guardianship records. These records can provide crucial information about the children and the relatives who cared for them.

Accessing Probate Records: County Courthouses and Archival Repositories

Probate records, like land records, were historically created and maintained at a local level, typically by a court with jurisdiction over estate matters. Accessing these records often involves researching in courthouses or archival repositories, although an increasing number are being digitized.

The location of probate records varies by country and jurisdiction:

1. **United States:**
    - **County Level:** In most US states, probate records are handled at the county level, usually by a Probate Court, Orphans' Court, Surrogate's Court, or a similar court. Records are typically held in the county courthouse or the county archives.

- **State Archives:** State archives may hold older county probate records that have been transferred from the courthouses.
- **Online Databases:** Major genealogy platforms, including Ancestry, FamilySearch, Fold3, and MyHeritage, have digitized significant collections of probate records for various U.S. counties and states. FamilySearch has an extensive and growing collection of digitized county probate records, often available for free browsing.

2. **United Kingdom:**
   - **England and Wales:** Before 1858, probate was handled by ecclesiastical courts (Church of England). Records from these courts are held in various locations, including The National Archives (PCC - Prerogative Court of Canterbury, which handled wealthier individuals) and local county record offices (for Consistory Courts and Archdeaconry Courts). From 1858 onwards, probate became a civil matter, handled by the Principal Probate Registry and District Probate Registries. Indexes to these civil probate records (National Probate Calendar) are widely available online, and copies of wills can be ordered.
   - **Scotland:** Probate records (Confirmations) are held by the National Records of Scotland and Sheriff Courts. Indexes and records are available on ScotlandsPeople (pay-per-view).

- **Ireland:** Probate records have a complex history due to political divisions and record losses. Ecclesiastical courts often held earlier records. From 1858, civil probate records were created. Records are held by the Public Record Office of Northern Ireland (PRONI) and the National Archives of Ireland. Many Irish probate records were destroyed in the 1922 Four Courts fire, but abstracts and indexes created before the fire are invaluable.

Accessing Records in Person:

- **Plan Your Visit:** Research the specific court or archive that holds the records you need. Check their website for hours, location, and any requirements for researchers.
- **Understand Their Indexing System:** Probate records are typically indexed by the name of the deceased and the year the probate was initiated. Learn how to use their indexes (which might be in physical volumes, on microfilm, or in a digital database).
- **Request the File or Book:** Once you find an entry in the index, you will need to request the physical file or the deed book containing the record.
- **Be Prepared to Spend Time:** Probate records can be lengthy and require careful reading and interpretation.

Accessing Records Online:

- **Search Online Indexes:** Start by searching online probate indexes on major genealogy platforms or archival websites.
- **Browse Digitized Collections:** If indexes are unavailable or incomplete, browse digitized collections of probate records, organized by court, record type, and date.
- **Utilize Online Finding Aids:** Websites of archives often have online catalogs or finding aids that describe their probate holdings.

Accessing probate records requires understanding the court system and record-keeping practices of the relevant time and place. Persistence in searching indexes and browsing collections is often necessary, but the genealogical rewards can be significant.

Understanding Legal Terminology: Deciphering the Language of Court Documents

Probate and court records are legal documents that often contain specialized terminology and archaic language, which can be challenging for beginners to understand. Familiarizing yourself with general legal terms from the historical period you are researching is crucial for accurate interpretation.

1. **Common Probate Terms:**
   - **Testator:** A person who has made a will.

- **Intestate:** Dying without a valid will.
- **Executor:** A person named in a will to carry out its terms.
- **Administrator:** A person appointed by the court to settle the estate of someone who died intestate.
- **Heir/Beneficiary/Legatee:** A person who inherits property from an estate.
- **Devise:** A gift of real property (land) in a will.
- **Bequest:** A gift of personal property (movable possessions) in a will.
- **Probate:** The legal process of proving a will and settling an estate.
- **Administration:** The legal process of settling an intestate estate.
- **Inventory:** A list of the deceased's personal property.
- **Appraisal:** The valuation of the deceased's property.
- **Account:** A record of the income and expenses of the estate.
- **Guardian:** A person appointed to care for minor children or manage their property.
- **Surety:** A person who co-signs a bond, guaranteeing that the executor or administrator will fulfill their duties.

2. **Archaic Language and Spelling:** Historical legal documents frequently employ older

forms of words, alternative spellings, and occasionally Latin phrases.

- **Consult Historical Dictionaries and Glossaries:** Use resources that define archaic words and legal terms from the relevant period. Online genealogical glossaries can be very helpful.
- **Context is Key:** Use the surrounding words and the overall purpose of the document to help you infer the meaning of unfamiliar terms.

3. **Handwriting:** As with other historical records, deciphering old handwriting is often necessary when working with probate and court records. Practice reading different styles of script.

4. **Standard Legal Phrases:** Legal documents often contain standardized phrases and clauses. While the exact wording may vary, recognizing these common elements can help you navigate the document.

5. **Numbers and Dates:** Pay close attention to how numbers and dates are written in historical documents.

Tips for Deciphering:

- **Read Slowly and Carefully:** Don't rush through the document. Take your time to examine each word and phrase.
- **Transcribe Difficult Sections:** If you are struggling with a particular section, try transcribing it word for word, even if you don't understand every

word initially. This can help you decipher the handwriting.

- **Compare with Other Documents:** If you find similar phrases or terms in other records you have accessed, compare them to help with interpretation.
- **Seek Assistance:** If you are truly stuck, ask for help from experienced genealogists in online forums or genealogical societies.

Understanding the language of probate and court records requires patience and a willingness to learn. However, the information contained within these documents is often so valuable that the effort is well rewarded.

Court Records Beyond Probate: Lawsuits, Criminal Proceedings, and Other Actions

While probate records are the most commonly used court records in genealogy, other types of court documents can also contain valuable information about your ancestors, revealing details about their interactions with the legal system and their community.

1. **Civil Lawsuits:** Records of lawsuits between individuals can reveal relationships (e.g., a lawsuit between siblings over an inheritance), business dealings, debts, and disputes with neighbors or other community members.

- **Genealogical Value:** Provides proof of individuals being in a specific location at a certain time, names individuals involved in the lawsuit (plaintiffs, defendants, witnesses), and details about the nature of the dispute, which can offer insights into your ancestors' lives and relationships.

2. **Criminal Proceedings:** Records of criminal trials can document ancestors who were accused of crimes, either as defendants, victims, or witnesses.

    - **Genealogical Value:** Places individuals in a specific location at a certain time. Can provide physical descriptions (in warrants or court descriptions), details about their activities, and names of associates or witnesses. While potentially sensitive, these records are part of an ancestor's history.

3. **Bastardy Bonds and Records:** Records related to children born outside of marriage. These can name the mother and the presumed father, providing crucial information for tracing illegitimate lines.

    - **Genealogical Value:** Direct proof of parentage in cases where other records are absent.

4. **Guardianship Records (Separate from Probate):** Courts sometimes appointed guardians for minor children even if there was no inheritance

involved, perhaps due to a parent's inability to care for them.
- ○ **Genealogical Value:** Names minor children and the appointed guardian, often indicating a familial relationship.

5. **Apprenticeship Records:** Court records sometimes documented the apprenticeship of young people to learn a trade.
- ○ **Genealogical Value:** Names the child and the master they were apprenticed to, placing them in a specific location and providing clues about their occupation.

6. **Divorce Records:** Records related to divorce proceedings can provide information about the dissolution of a marriage, including the names of spouses and children, and sometimes the reasons for the divorce.
- ○ **Genealogical Value:** Confirms a divorce and names the individuals involved.

7. **Coroner's Inquests:** Records of investigations into deaths that were sudden, unexpected, or potentially unnatural.
- ○ **Genealogical Value:** Provides details about the deceased, the circumstances of their death, and the names of witnesses. It can sometimes provide a more precise death date or location than a death certificate.

Accessing Other Court Records:
- **County Courthouses and Archives:** Many of these records were created at the county

level and are held in courthouses or county archives.

- **State Archives:** State archives may hold copies of court records or records from higher state courts.
- **National Archives:** The National Archives hold records from federal courts.
- **Online Databases:** The availability of digitized court records online is increasing, but is less comprehensive than for census or vital records. FamilySearch is actively digitizing various types of court records.

Exploring court records beyond probate can be more challenging due to the variety of record types and indexing systems. Still, they can provide unique and valuable insights into your ancestors' lives and legal interactions.

Using Court Records to Prove Relationships and Solve Problems

Probate and other court records are powerful tools for proving genealogical relationships and breaking down difficult brick walls. The explicit statements of relationship found in wills, administration papers, and guardianship records provide direct evidence that can confirm connections when other records are ambiguous or missing.

1. **Direct Proof of Relationships:**

- **Wills:** "to my son, John," "to my daughter, Mary Smith (wife of Thomas Smith)," "to the children of my deceased daughter, Sarah."
- **Administrations:** Petitions for administration stating the relationship of the petitioner to the deceased (e.g., "petition of Mary Smith, widow of John Smith"). The court orders the distribution of property to "the children and legal heirs of the deceased."
- **Guardianships:** Records appointing a guardian to the "minor children of John Smith," often naming the guardian and their relationship (e.g., "guardian appointed: Thomas Jones, brother of the deceased John Smith").
- **Lawsuits:** A lawsuit between named individuals explicitly stating their relationship (e.g., "John Smith vs. Thomas Smith, his brother").

2. **Resolving Conflicting Evidence:** If other records (like census entries with inconsistent relationships) provide conflicting information, a clear statement of relationship in a probate or court record can help resolve the conflict and establish the correct connection.

3. **Identifying Missing Individuals:** Administration records, in particular, are valuable for identifying all legal heirs, including children who may have died young or not been consistently listed

in census records. Guardianship records are crucial for identifying minor children after a parent's death.

4. **Connecting Families Through Legal Interactions:** Court records, even civil lawsuits or criminal proceedings, can name individuals who interacted with your ancestor. Researching these individuals (applying the FAN principle) can sometimes reveal familial connections or associations.

5. **Using Witnesses and Sureties:** Individuals who served as witnesses to wills or sureties on probate or guardianship bonds were often family members or close associates. Researching their records can help you identify potential relatives and expand your research network.

6. **Understanding Property Distribution and Inheritance:** Probate records reveal how property was passed down through generations, which is closely tied to family structure and relationships.

Court records often provide the "smoking gun" – the explicit piece of evidence that directly proves a familial connection. They require careful searching and interpretation, but the rewards in terms of confirmed relationships and broken brick walls can be immense.

Case Studies in Court Records: Unlocking Difficult Ancestral Connections

Examining real-life examples of how probate and court records have been used to solve genealogical puzzles can illustrate their power.

- **Proving the Father of a Child:** A researcher has a birth record for John Smith that only lists his mother, Mary Smith. They find the probate file for Thomas Smith, who died shortly before John's birth. The inventory includes a payment to "Mary Smith for the maintenance of my son, John." This, combined with other circumstantial evidence (such as Mary inheriting from Thomas's estate), can strongly suggest that Thomas Smith was John's father, even without a father's name being listed on the birth certificate.
- **Identifying All Children of an Intestate Couple:** A researcher knows a couple had several children from census records, but isn't sure if they've identified all of them. They find the administration records for the father's estate. The court orders for the distribution of the estate list all the legal heirs, including daughters who had married and left home (listed with their married names), and potentially children who died as minors whose share passed to their siblings. This provides a complete list of the legal children at the time of the father's death.
- **Connecting Families Through a Guardianship:** A researcher is trying to connect

their ancestor, Sarah Jones, to her potential father, Thomas Jones. They find guardianship records for the minor children of a deceased William Brown. The guardian appointed is Thomas Jones, identified in the record as "the uncle of the said minor children." This provides strong evidence that William Brown's wife was a sister of Thomas Jones. If William Brown's wife was indeed Sarah, as other records suggest, then Thomas Jones was likely Sarah's father or uncle, depending on the precise relationship stated.

These case studies demonstrate that exploring probate and court records, even when no will is immediately apparent, can provide crucial evidence for confirming relationships, identifying individuals, and breaking down genealogical brick walls. These records offer a unique perspective on your ancestors' lives, their families, and their interactions within the legal framework of their time. Don't overlook the power of the courthouse in your ancestry detective work.

Chapter 11: Leveraging DNA Testing: Understanding and Using Genetic Genealogy

You've honed your skills as an ancestry detective, learning to unearth clues from vital records, census data, migration patterns, military service, land ownership, and court documents. You've built a framework of your family history based on paper trails and oral traditions. Now, prepare to add a powerful new tool to your detective kit – your own DNA.

In recent years, direct-to-consumer DNA testing has revolutionized genealogical research. It offers a unique way to connect with living relatives you never knew you had, confirm relationships found through documents, and sometimes even break through stubborn brick walls where the paper trail has gone cold. Your DNA carries a biological record of your ancestry, a story written in your genes, and by comparing your DNA to that of others, you can unlock new avenues of discovery about your family's past.

However, DNA testing is not a magic bullet that will instantly reveal your entire family tree. It is a powerful *tool* that complements, rather than replaces, traditional documentary research. Understanding how DNA is inherited, what the different types of tests reveal, how to interpret your results, and how to use DNA evidence in conjunction with your documentary findings is crucial for leveraging its full potential in your ancestry detective work.

This chapter will guide you through the basics of genetic genealogy, helping you understand your DNA results and use them effectively to expand and verify your family history.

The Genetic Revolution: Incorporating DNA into Your Research

For decades, genealogical research relied almost entirely on historical documents. While these records remain fundamental, the advent of affordable and accessible DNA testing has added a new dimension to the field. Genetic genealogy utilizes DNA analysis to aid in identifying relatives and inferring ancestral relationships.

How does DNA fit into your ancestry detective work?

1. **Connecting with Living Relatives:** DNA testing companies compare your DNA to the DNA of millions of other individuals in their databases. When you share significant amounts of DNA with another person, it indicates that you are related. These DNA matches can be close relatives (siblings, cousins) or more distant cousins you never knew you had. Connecting with these matches can lead to sharing information, documents, and even breaking down brick walls on shared ancestral lines.

2. **Confirming Documentary Research:** DNA evidence can be used to confirm relationships you've found through traditional records. If you believe, based on documents, that two individuals were siblings, and their descendants (who have tested) show a level of shared DNA consistent with a cousin relationship, it provides strong support for your documentary findings.

3. **Breaking Down Brick Walls:** When the paper trail ends, DNA can sometimes provide the clues needed to move forward. By identifying DNA matches on a challenging line of your tree and analyzing your shared ancestors, you can sometimes identify a common ancestor or a previously unknown connection that helps you push back another generation.

4. **Inferring Ethnicity and Ancestral Origins:** DNA testing provides an "ethnicity estimate," which attempts to identify the regions of the world where your ancestors likely lived based on patterns in your DNA compared to reference populations. While these estimates should be viewed as just that – estimates – they can sometimes provide clues about ancestral origins that were previously unknown.

5. **Exploring Maternal and Paternal Lines (with specific tests):** While autosomal DNA tests provide information about all your ancestral lines, Y-DNA and mitochondrial DNA (mtDNA) tests can provide specific information about your direct paternal line (father's father's

father, etc.) and direct maternal line (mother's mother's mother, etc.), respectively.

The integration of DNA into genealogical research has opened up exciting new possibilities. It allows us to connect with our biological past tangibly and provides a powerful tool for complementing and enhancing traditional documentary research. Think of DNA as another type of record, a biological record, that needs to be interpreted and used in conjunction with the paper trail.

Types of DNA Tests: Autosomal, Y-DNA, and mtDNA

There are three main types of DNA tests commonly used in genetic genealogy, each providing different kinds of information and tracing different lines of your ancestry. Understanding these differences is crucial for choosing the proper test(s) for your research goals.

1. **Autosomal DNA (atDNA):**
    - **What it tests:** Autosomal DNA is the DNA found on the 22 pairs of numbered chromosomes (autosomes). It is inherited from *all* of your ancestors, both maternal and paternal lines, in relatively random segments.
    - **What it reveals:**
        - **Ethnicity Estimates:** Provides an estimate of your ancestral origins by comparing segments of your autosomal

DNA to reference populations around the world.
- **DNA Matches:** Identifies living relatives with whom you share a significant amount of autosomal DNA, indicating a recent common ancestor. The amount of shared DNA (measured in centimorgans, cM) helps estimate the degree of closeness in the relationship.
  - **Inheritance Pattern:** You inherit approximately 50% of your autosomal DNA from each parent, who inherited 50% from each of their parents, and so on. However, the *specific segments* of DNA you inherit from more distant ancestors are random. This means you may not inherit enough DNA from *every* distant ancestor to be detectable through autosomal testing. Autosomal DNA is most helpful in identifying relatives within about 5-6 generations.
  - **Who can take it:** Both men and women can take autosomal DNA tests.
  - **Most Common Use:** Finding living relatives and estimating recent ancestral origins.

2. **Y-Chromosome DNA (Y-DNA):**
    - **What it tests:** Y-DNA is found only on the Y chromosome, which is passed down almost unchanged from father to son through the generations.
    - **What it reveals:**
        - **Paternal Line Ancestry:** Traces your direct paternal line (father's father's father, etc.).

- **Y-DNA Haplotype/Haplogroup:** Identifies your Y-DNA profile, which can be compared to others to see if you share a common paternal ancestor. A haplogroup represents a large group of men who share a distant common paternal ancestor.
  - **Inheritance Pattern:** Passed directly from father to son. Only males have a Y chromosome.
  - **Who can take it:** Only males can take Y-DNA tests. Females interested in their direct paternal line would need to ask their father, brother, paternal uncle, or paternal male cousin to test.
  - **Most Common Use:** Tracing a surname's history (as surnames often follow the paternal line), confirming paternal lineage, and connecting with other males who share a common paternal ancestor. Y-DNA is useful for tracing ancestry much further back in time than autosomal DNA, sometimes hundreds or even thousands of years, for deeper ancestry. However, for recent genealogy, it's most helpful in confirming paternal lines where other records are missing.

3. **Mitochondrial DNA (mtDNA):**
   - **What it tests:** mtDNA is found in the mitochondria, which are organelles within cells. mtDNA is passed down almost unchanged from mother to child, by both sons and daughters.
   - **What it reveals:**

- **Maternal Line Ancestry:** Traces your direct maternal line (mother's mother's mother, etc.).
- **mtDNA Haplogroup:** Identifies your mtDNA profile, which can be compared to others to see if you share a common maternal ancestor. An mtDNA haplogroup represents a large group of people who share a distant common maternal ancestor.

- **Inheritance Pattern:** Passed directly from mother to all of her children (sons and daughters).
- **Who can take it:** Both men and women can take mtDNA tests.
- **Most Common Use:** Tracing a direct maternal line where the surname changes each generation (as it follows the female line), confirming maternal lineage, and connecting with others who share a common maternal ancestor. mtDNA mutates very slowly, making it most helpful in tracing ancient maternal ancestry or confirming maternal lines where other records are missing in more recent generations. However, it identifies fewer matches than autosomal DNA for recent genealogy.

Which Test Should You Start With?

For most beginners in genealogical research, the **autosomal DNA test** is the best place to start. It provides the broadest view of your recent ancestry, connects you with the most significant number of living relatives (DNA matches) across all your ancestral lines, and includes the ethnicity estimate, which is often a point of curiosity for beginners. Y-DNA and mtDNA tests are more specialized and are typically pursued later to answer specific questions about direct paternal or maternal lines.

Choosing a DNA Testing Company: Comparing Services and Databases

Once you've decided which type of DNA test to take (most likely autosomal to start), you need to choose a testing company. Several major companies offer direct-to-consumer DNA testing, each with its strengths, weaknesses, database size, and features. The size and diversity of the company's database are crucial, as you can only match with individuals who have tested with the same company or uploaded their results to a compatible platform.

The major players in autosomal DNA testing include:
1. **AncestryDNA (ancestry.com):**
    - **Database Size:** The most extensive database of autosomal DNA test takers globally, meaning you are likely to get the most DNA matches here.
    - **Strengths:** Large database, integrates seamlessly with Ancestry's extensive record collections and online family trees (allowing you to see common

ancestors with matches if you link your tree), provides ethnicity estimates, and features like Thrulines (which suggest potential connections to matches based on trees).
- **Weaknesses:** Requires an Ancestry subscription to access some features and contact all matches. Cannot upload raw DNA data from other companies directly to their primary matching database (though some third-party tools can analyze AncestryDNA data).

2. **23andMe (23andme.com):**
   - **Database Size:** A large database, though smaller than AncestryDNA for genealogical purposes.
   - **Strengths:** Offers health reports in addition to ancestry information (though health reports require a separate or higher-tier purchase). Provides a detailed ethnicity breakdown. Shows DNA segments shared with matches. Allows you to see how much DNA you share with matches on specific chromosomes.
   - **Weaknesses:** The Interface is perhaps less geared towards traditional genealogical research compared to AncestryDNA. Cannot upload raw DNA data from other companies.

3. **MyHeritage DNA (myheritage.com):**
   - **Database Size:** A significant and growing database, particularly strong with test takers from Europe and other

international locations, which can be valuable for connecting with relatives outside of North America.
- ○ **Strengths:** Good for connecting with international relatives. Integrates with MyHeritage's record collections and online family trees. Allows you to upload raw DNA data from AncestryDNA or 23andMe for free matching within their database (though some advanced features may require a subscription). Offers ethnicity estimates and genetic groups.
- ○ **Weaknesses:** Database size is smaller than AncestryDNA overall, though strong in certain regions.

4. **FamilyTreeDNA (familytreedna.com):**
- ○ **Database Size:** Smaller than the major players for autosomal DNA, but a strong choice if you are interested in Y-DNA or mtDNA testing, as they are a leader in these areas.
- ○ **Strengths:** Offers all three types of DNA tests (autosomal, Y-DNA, and mtDNA). Strong in Y-DNA and mtDNA analysis and matching. Allows uploading raw autosomal DNA data from other companies for matching. Offers surname projects for Y-DNA research.
- ○ **Weaknesses:** The Autosomal database is smaller than AncestryDNA or MyHeritage.

5. **Living DNA (livingdna.com):**

- **Database Size:** Smaller database compared to the major players.
- **Strengths:** Offers detailed ethnicity estimates, particularly for the UK and Ireland. Offers all three types of DNA tests. Allows uploading raw autosomal DNA data from other companies for free matching.
- **Weaknesses:** Smaller match database limits the number of potential relative connections.

Choosing the Best Company for You:

- **For the most DNA matches (autosomal):** AncestryDNA currently has the largest database.
- **For connecting with European relatives (autosomal):** MyHeritage DNA is often recommended due to its database demographics.
- **For free matching (autosomal):** FamilySearch allows you to link DNA results from several companies to your tree, and some companies (MyHeritage, FamilyTreeDNA, Living DNA) allow free uploads of raw data from other companies for matching.
- **For Y-DNA or mtDNA testing:** FamilyTreeDNA is a leading provider.
- **If your primary interest is UK/Ireland ethnicity,** Living DNA specializes in this.

Many experienced genealogists recommend testing with **AncestryDNA** for the most significant number of matches and then downloading your raw DNA data to upload it to other compatible platforms, such as MyHeritage DNA and FamilyTreeDNA, to maximize your potential match pool. This is often the most cost-effective way to get a broad range of matches.

Understanding Your Results: Ethnicity Estimates and DNA Matches

Once you receive your DNA results, the first things you'll typically see are your ethnicity estimate and a list of your DNA matches. Understanding what these mean is your first step in leveraging your DNA for genealogy.

1. **Ethnicity Estimates:**
    - **What they are:** These are estimates of the percentage of your DNA that comes from different geographical regions or populations around the world.
    - **How they are generated:** Companies compare segments of your DNA to "reference panels" – collections of DNA samples from individuals with known, long-term ancestry in specific regions. Based on how much your DNA matches the patterns in these reference panels, they estimate your ancestral origins.
    - **Interpretation:** Ethnicity estimates are just that – *estimates*. They are based on probabilities and the company's specific reference panels and algorithms. Different companies may provide slightly different estimates due to variations in their methods and

reference populations. Ethnicity estimates are generally more accurate for broader regions than for particular localities, especially further back in time. They are best viewed as a guide or a starting point for further research, rather than definitive proof of ancestry in a particular region. As company databases and algorithms improve, your ethnicity estimate may change over time.

- **Genealogical Value:** While not precise for specific ancestors, ethnicity estimates can sometimes confirm known ancestral origins or suggest potential origins in areas you hadn't previously considered, prompting new research avenues.

2. **DNA Matches (Genetic Relatives):**
    - **What they are:** A list of other individuals in the company's database with whom you share a significant amount of DNA.
    - **Information Provided:** For each match, you'll typically see:
        - Their username or name.
        - The estimated relationship (e.g., 1st cousin, 3rd cousin, 4th-6th cousin).
        - The amount of shared DNA (measured in centimorgans, cM, and sometimes as a percentage).
        - The number of shared DNA segments.
        - Often, a comparison of your ethnicity estimates.
        - Potentially, a link to their family tree (if they have one and have shared it).

- **Interpretation:** The amount of shared DNA is the most important factor for estimating the closeness of the relationship. Larger amounts of shared DNA indicate closer relationships. Companies provide charts or guides showing the typical ranges of shared DNA for different relationship types (e.g., first cousins typically share around 850 cM, while fourth cousins share a much smaller amount). However, there are overlapping ranges for different relationships, especially for more distant cousins, so the estimated relationship is just a guide.
- **Genealogical Value:** DNA matches are incredibly valuable for connecting with living relatives, confirming known relationships, and identifying potential common ancestors.

Understanding both your ethnicity estimate (as a broad guide) and, more importantly, your DNA matches (as concrete connections to living relatives) is your starting point for using DNA in your genealogical research.

Working with DNA Matches: Identifying Common Ancestors and Confirming Relationships

Your list of DNA matches is your network of genetic relatives. The goal is to work with these matches to identify your shared ancestors and use this information to expand and verify your family tree. This is where the real detective work with DNA begins.

1. **Focus on Closer Matches First:** Start by examining your closest matches (2nd cousins and closer). These individuals share a more recent common ancestor with you, making it easier to identify that ancestor.

2. **Examine Shared Matches:** Most companies provide a "shared matches" or "in common with" tool. This allows you to select a match and see all the other matches you *both* share. Matches who are "in common with" each other and with you likely descend from a common ancestral couple or family group. This is a fundamental tool for clustering your matches and identifying the branches of your family to which they belong.

3. **Compare Family Trees:** If your DNA matches have linked family trees to their DNA results, compare their trees to your own to look for common ancestors. If you share a common ancestor, it helps confirm the relationship and places the match within a specific branch of your tree. If they have ancestors in their tree that you don't, and you share a significant amount of DNA, those individuals are potential ancestors for you to research.

4. **Build Quick & Dirty Trees for Matches Without Trees:** If a match doesn't have a tree, try to build a small "quick and dirty" tree for them based on public records (census, vital records, obituaries) to try and identify their recent

ancestors. This can help you find the common ancestor you share.

5. **Contact Your Matches:** Reach out to your DNA matches, especially closer ones, to introduce yourself, explain your connection (based on shared DNA and potential common ancestors in trees), and offer to share information. Be polite, patient, and respectful of their privacy. Some individuals may be very interested in genealogy, while others may have primarily tested for ethnicity and may not be actively researching.

6. **Analyze the Amount of Shared DNA:** Use shared cM amounts and the number of shared segments to estimate the possible relationships. Use online tools and charts to help you understand the probability of different relationships based on shared DNA.

7. **Triangulate Shared Segments (More Advanced):** Some platforms and third-party tools allow you to see the specific segments of DNA you share with your matches. If you and two or more matches all share a DNA segment on the same chromosome in the exact location, it indicates that you all inherited that segment from a recent common ancestor. This "triangulation" can provide strong evidence for a shared ancestral line.

8. **Cluster Your Matches:** Use the shared matches tool to group your matches into clusters. Each cluster likely represents descendants of a specific ancestral couple or

family group. This helps you sort your matches and focus your research on particular branches of your tree. Tools like the Leeds Method, a manual clustering technique, can be helpful.

Working with DNA matches is an ongoing process. As more people test, you will get new matches. By systematically analyzing your matches, comparing trees, using shared matches, and contacting your genetic relatives, you can leverage your DNA to expand your family tree and connect with previously unknown cousins.

Using Third-Party Tools: Enhancing Your DNA Analysis

While the major testing companies provide their tools for analyzing your DNA results and working with matches, several third-party websites and tools can enhance your analysis and provide additional insights, particularly by allowing you to upload your raw DNA data from multiple companies.

1. **GEDmatch (gedmatch.com):**
    - **What it is:** A free, non-profit website that allows users to upload their raw DNA data from most major testing companies (AncestryDNA, 23andMe, MyHeritage DNA, FamilyTreeDNA, Living DNA). Its primary function is to allow you to compare your DNA with individuals who have tested with different companies, significantly expanding your potential match pool.

- **Strengths:** Allows cross-company comparisons, has various analysis tools (including one-to-one comparisons, one-to-many comparisons, and tools for analyzing shared segments and triangulation), and provides ethnicity estimates from different models.
- **Weaknesses:** Interface can be less user-friendly for beginners. Primarily focused on DNA analysis, not integrated with record collections.

2. **DNA Painter (dnapainter.com):**
   - **What it is:** A website that allows you to "paint" or visualize the segments of DNA you share with your matches onto a representation of your chromosomes. You manually enter information about your matches and the segments you share (often obtained from GEDmatch or company websites that provide segment data).
   - **Strengths:** Powerful visualization tool for understanding which segments of DNA come from which ancestors. Helps identify clusters of matches that triangulate on the same segment. Helpful in confirming ancestral lines and breaking down brick walls by seeing which ancestors contributed specific segments.
   - **Weaknesses:** Requires manual input of data. Requires understanding of shared DNA segments.
3. **Other Third-Party Tools:** Various smaller websites and tools offer specialized DNA analysis features, including tools for clustering matches,

estimating relationships based on shared DNA, and visualizing ancestral paths.

How to Use Third-Party Tools:
- **Download Your Raw DNA Data:** Once you've tested with a major company, you can usually download your raw DNA data file from their website.
- **Upload to Compatible Platforms:** Upload your raw data to GEDmatch, MyHeritage DNA, FamilyTreeDNA, and Living DNA (check their compatibility requirements) to expand your match pool.
- **Explore Analysis Tools:** Experiment with the different analysis tools offered by these platforms to gain deeper insights into your DNA and your matches.
- **Use Visualization Tools:** Tools like DNA Painter can help you organize and understand your matches and the segments you share.

Third-party tools can significantly enhance your DNA analysis, particularly for connecting with matches from different companies and for more advanced techniques like triangulation and segment analysis. While not essential for basic DNA genealogy, they are valuable resources for the more experienced ancestry detective.

Building and Using a Shared Matches Matrix: Visualizing DNA Connections

One of the most powerful techniques for organizing and analyzing your DNA matches is building a Shared Matches Matrix, also known as a cluster chart. This method helps you visually group your matches into clusters that likely represent descendants of specific ancestral couples or family groups.

How to Build a Shared Matches Matrix (Leeds Method - a simple manual approach):

1. **Select a Starting Set of Matches:** Begin with your autosomal DNA matches in a certain cM range (e.g., 400 cM down to 100 cM, or a similar range that focuses on likely 3rd and 4th cousins). Avoid very close matches initially, as they connect to multiple recent lines.

2. **Create a Spreadsheet or Grid:** Create a spreadsheet or draw a grid. List your selected matches along the top row and down the first column.

3. **Identify Shared Matches:** For each match on your list, use the "shared matches" or "in common with" tool provided by the testing company to see which other matches *from your initial list* they also share DNA with.

4. **Mark Shared Matches in the Grid:** In your spreadsheet or grid, mark an "X" or a color in the cell where two matches intersect if they are also shared matches.

5. **Identify Clusters:** Look for groups of matches that consistently share DNA (forming blocks of "X"s or colors in the grid). Each of these clusters likely represents descendants of a specific ancestral couple (one of your 2x great-grandparents, for example).

6. **Assign Clusters to Ancestral Lines (if known):** If you can identify a common ancestor for some of the matches in a cluster (by comparing trees or through communication), you can assign that entire cluster to that ancestral line.

7. **Analyze Unassigned Clusters:** Clusters that you cannot immediately assign to a known ancestral line represent a branch of your tree where you have a brick wall or less documented ancestry. These are prime targets for focused research.

Benefits of Using a Shared Matches Matrix:
- **Organizes Matches:** Helps you make sense of a long list of DNA matches by grouping them into logical clusters.
- **Identifies Ancestral Lines:** Helps you determine which branches of your family your matches belong to.
- **Highlights Brick Walls:** Clusters that cannot be assigned to a known line point to areas where you need to focus your documentary research.
- **Facilitates Collaboration:** Helps you identify groups of relatives who are researching the same ancestral lines.
- **Visualizes Connections:** Provides a clear visual representation of how your matches are related to each other and you.

Building and using a Shared Matches Matrix is a powerful technique for organizing your DNA match data and strategically focusing your research efforts. Various online tools can also automate this process.

Applying DNA to Solve Genealogical Puzzles: Breaking Down Brick Walls

DNA evidence can be a powerful tool for overcoming genealogical brick walls – those points in your research where the documentary trail has gone cold and you cannot identify an ancestor or a relationship. By combining DNA analysis with traditional research techniques, you can sometimes find the clues needed to push back another generation.

How DNA Helps Break Down Brick Walls:

1. **Identifying Unknown Ancestors:** If you have a brick wall (e.g., you don't know the father of your great-grandfather), identify DNA matches who descend from that uncertain ancestral line (by using shared matches and analyzing their trees). By examining the common ancestors of these matches, you might identify individuals who are potential ancestors for your brick wall line.

2. **Confirming Hypotheses:** If you have a hypothesis about a potential ancestor or relationship based on circumstantial documentary evidence, finding DNA matches who fit that hypothesized connection can provide strong support for your theory.

3. **Discovering Previously Unknown Relatives:** Connecting with DNA matches may reveal previously unknown siblings, half-siblings, or cousins, which can open up entirely new avenues of research and lead to the discovery of unknown ancestral lines.

4. **Using Surname Projects (Y-DNA):** If your brick wall is on a direct paternal line and you suspect a particular surname, participating in a Y-DNA surname project for that name can

connect you with other males who share that surname and a common paternal ancestor, potentially revealing your ancestral connection.

5. **Geographical Clustering of Matches:** Sometimes, a cluster of DNA matches without trees can be linked to a specific geographical area based on their stated locations. This suggests that your shared ancestry is connected to that region, guiding your documentary research to local records.

6. **Analyzing Ethnicity Estimates (with Caution):** While not precise, a strong ethnicity signal in your DNA that differs from your known ancestry might suggest a hidden ancestral line from that region, prompting you to explore immigration records or records from that area.

Strategies for Using DNA to Break Down Brick Walls:

- **Test Multiple Family Members:** Encourage older generations and individuals on different branches of your family tree to test. Their DNA is closer to the common ancestors and can provide more definitive connections.
- **Upload Your Raw Data to Multiple Platforms:** Maximize your match pool by uploading your data to compatible sites.
- **Utilize Shared Matches and Clustering Techniques:** Group your matches to identify the ancestral lines they represent, particularly focusing on clusters that connect to your brick wall.

- **Build Out Trees for Your Matches:** Don't just look at their reported trees. Use public records to build out trees for your matches, especially those who are closer relatives, to identify potential common ancestors.
- **Collaborate with Matches:** Communicate with your matches, share information, and work together to identify common ancestors.
- **Combine DNA Evidence with Documentary Research:** DNA provides clues and confirms relationships, but documentary research is essential for verifying the information and building a complete picture. Use DNA hints to guide your search for records.

Breaking down brick walls with DNA requires a combination of genetic analysis, traditional research skills, and collaboration with your DNA matches. It's a challenging but often gratifying aspect of genetic genealogy.

The Ethics of DNA Testing: Privacy, Unexpected Discoveries, and Informed Consent

As you venture into the world of genetic genealogy, it is crucial to be mindful of the ethical considerations involved. DNA testing can reveal sensitive information, lead to unexpected discoveries, and has implications for the privacy of not only your genetic information but also that of your relatives.

1. **Privacy:**
   - **Your Privacy:** Consider how comfortable you are with a private company storing your genetic information and potentially using it for research purposes (as outlined in their terms of service). Understand their privacy policies and how they handle your data.
   - **The Privacy of Your Relatives:** When you test, you are also providing information about your living relatives, as you share DNA with them. Be mindful of this and avoid sharing sensitive information about living individuals without their consent. Consider the privacy settings of your online family tree.
   - **Law Enforcement Access:** Be aware that some DNA testing companies may cooperate with law enforcement requests for access to their databases (though policies vary between companies). Understand the company's stance on this issue if it is a concern for you.
2. **Unexpected Discoveries:** DNA testing can sometimes reveal unexpected or sensitive family information, such as:
   - **Previously Unknown Siblings or Parents:** Discovering you have half-siblings or that the person you believed was your parent is not biologically related.
   - **Misattributed Parentage:** Discovering that a presumed paternal or maternal line is incorrect.

- **Undisclosed Adoptions:** Uncovering adoptions that were not previously known.
- **Genetic Health Information:** While most ancestry tests don't provide comprehensive health reports, some may offer limited health-related information or links to health services.

Be emotionally prepared for the possibility of unexpected discoveries and consider how you will handle them with sensitivity and respect for all individuals involved.

3. **Informed Consent:**
   - **For Yourself:** Read and understand the terms of service and privacy policy of the DNA testing company before purchasing a test.
   - **For Relatives:** If you are encouraging or facilitating DNA testing for other family members, ensure they fully understand what the test involves, what kind of information it might reveal, and how their data will be used and stored. Obtain their informed consent *before* they test. This is particularly important for older or vulnerable relatives.

4. **Managing Sensitive Information:** If you uncover sensitive family information through DNA testing, exercise discretion and sensitivity in how you handle and share that information. Consider the potential impact on living individuals.

5. **Communicating with Matches:** When contacting DNA matches, be polite, respectful, and understand that they may have different levels of interest in genealogy or different reasons for testing.

Respect their decision if they do not wish to engage.

The ethical landscape of genetic genealogy is still evolving. By being informed, respecting privacy, and handling discoveries with sensitivity, you can navigate this landscape responsibly and ensure that your pursuit of family history is conducted ethically.

Integrating DNA Findings with Documentary Evidence: Building a More Complete Picture

DNA evidence and documentary research are not separate paths; they are two complementary tools that, when used together, can build a more complete, accurate, and compelling picture of your family history. DNA provides clues and confirms relationships, while documents provide the names, dates, places, and stories that flesh out the biological connections.

1. **Use DNA Clues to Guide Documentary Research:** If a cluster of DNA matches points to a specific geographical area or a potential common ancestor, use this information to focus your search for records in that location and period. DNA hints can provide direction when the paper trail is unclear.

2. **Use Documentary Research to Interpret DNA Matches:** Once you identify a DNA match, use documentary records (census, vital records, etc.) to build out their family tree and identify potential common ancestors. This helps you

understand your relationship to the match and which ancestral line you share.

3. **Corroborate Documentary Findings with DNA:** If you have documented a relationship through traditional records, use DNA evidence (comparing shared cM with expected ranges, or finding triangulated segments) to provide biological support for that relationship. This adds a layer of confidence to your findings.

4. **Resolve Conflicting Evidence:** In cases where documentary evidence is contradictory or unclear, DNA can sometimes provide the definitive proof needed to resolve the conflict and establish the correct relationship.

5. **Add DNA Information to Your Family Tree and Research Log:** Record information about your DNA matches, shared cM amounts, and potential common ancestors in your genealogy software or online tree. Note in your research log when DNA evidence was used to support a conclusion.

6. **Build Trees for Your Matches:** To effectively use your DNA matches, you will need to build at least basic trees for them using public records. This is a form of documentary research driven by DNA.

7. **Analyze Clusters and Ancestral Lines:** As you identify clusters of DNA matches belonging to specific ancestral lines (using the Shared Matches Matrix or similar tools), focus your documentary research on those lines to

identify common ancestors further and expand those branches of your tree.

8. **Recognize the Limitations of Each Tool:** Understand that documentary records can be incomplete or inaccurate, and DNA has limitations in tracing very distant ancestry or identifying precise relationships in some cases. Using both tools together helps mitigate their limitations.

Integrating DNA findings with documentary evidence is the most effective way to leverage the power of genetic genealogy. DNA can provide the sparks of connection and confirmation, while documents provide the fuel and structure to build a robust and well-supported family history. Embrace both tools in your ancestry detective work, and you will unlock a deeper and more accurate understanding of your family's past. With your knowledge of DNA basics and how to work with your results, you are now ready to consider how to compile and share your discoveries.

Charles Pembroke

Chapter 12: Weaving the Narrative: Writing and Sharing Your Family Story

You've embarked on an incredible journey as an ancestry detective. You've interviewed relatives, delved into dusty archives and online databases, navigated the complexities of vital records, deciphered census data, traced migrations, uncovered military service, explored land ownership, navigated court documents, and even unlocked clues in your very own DNA. You've gathered names, dates, places, and facts, meticulously recording your findings and building a structured family tree. But what do you do with all this information?

The true culmination of your ancestry detective work is not just the collection of data, but the weaving of that data into a narrative – a compelling story that brings your ancestors to life and shares their experiences with others. Your family history is more than just a list of names and dates on a chart; it's a rich tapestry of individual lives, shaped by historical events, personal choices, and the simple realities of everyday existence in times gone by. Sharing this story ensures that your ancestors are remembered and that their legacy lives on.

This chapter will guide you through the process of transforming your research findings into a written narrative and exploring various ways to share your family history with relatives and potentially a wider audience. It's time to move from detective work to storytelling and preservation.

Beyond the Names and Dates: Why Telling the Story Matters

You could present your family history as a series of charts and lists, and there is certainly value in that for organizational purposes. However, a list of names and dates, no matter how accurate or extensive, rarely captures the imagination or resonates deeply with others. What people connect with are stories – narratives of human experience, challenges overcome, joys celebrated, and lives lived.

Why is telling the story of your family history so important?

1. **Bringing Ancestors to Life:** Names and dates provide the framework, but stories add the color, texture, and depth that bring your ancestors to life as real people. Sharing anecdotes about their personalities, struggles, achievements, and daily routines makes them relatable and memorable.
2. **Connecting with Your Heritage:** Understanding the stories of your ancestors helps you understand your heritage and identity. It provides context for your own life and a sense of continuity with the past.
3. **Sharing with Family:** Family history is meant to be shared. Engagingly telling the story makes it accessible and enjoyable to relatives of all ages,

including younger generations who might not be captivated by raw genealogical data alone.

4. **Preserving Family Memories:** Oral traditions and family stories can fade over time. Writing down these narratives preserves them for future generations, complementing the factual information you have gathered from records.
5. **Understanding Historical Context:** By weaving your ancestors' lives into the broader fabric of history, you gain a deeper understanding of the times in which they lived. Their personal stories illustrate the impact of major historical events on individual lives.
6. **Creating a Lasting Legacy:** A written or digital family history narrative is a lasting legacy that you can pass down to your children, grandchildren, and beyond. It ensures that the knowledge and stories you have uncovered will not be lost.
7. **Inspiring Future Research:** A well-told family history can inspire other family members to become interested in their ancestry and continue the research journey.
8. **Finding Meaning in the Data:** The process of writing and telling the story helps you synthesize the vast amount of data you have collected, find patterns and connections, and identify the most meaningful aspects of your ancestors' lives.
9. **Honoring Your Ancestors:** By sharing their stories, you honor the lives and experiences of those who came before you, ensuring they are not forgotten.

10. **Making Research Accessible:** Presenting your research in a narrative format makes it more accessible and understandable to individuals who are not experienced genealogists.

Think of yourself as a historical biographer for your own family. You have gathered the raw materials, and now you are tasked with crafting a compelling narrative that captures the essence of their lives and shares it with the world (or at least your family).

Structuring Your Family History: Chronological, Topical, or Individual Stories

Once you're ready to start writing your family history narrative, you'll need to consider how to structure the information you've gathered. There are several common approaches, and the best one for you will depend on the scope of your research, the amount of information you have, and the story you want to tell. You can also combine these approaches.

1. **Chronological Structure (Moving Forward in Time):**
    - **How it works:** You start with the earliest known ancestors in a particular line or for a specific family group and tell their story moving forward through time, generation by generation, to the present day.
    - **Advantages:** Provides a clear and logical flow, making it easy for readers to follow the progression of the family through history. Allows

you to incorporate historical context for each generation.

    o **Disadvantages:** Can sometimes feel like just a string of biographies if you don't emphasize the connections and broader themes. It can become very long and complex if you are tracing many lines simultaneously.

    o **Best For:** Tracing a specific surname line or the descendants of a particular ancestral couple.

2. **Reverse Chronological Structure (Moving Backward in Time):**

    o **How it works:** You start with yourself and move backward in time, telling the story of your parents, then your grandparents, and so on.

    o **Advantages:** Starts with what is most familiar to the reader (you and recent generations). It can be a good way to introduce the research journey itself.

    o **Disadvantages:** Can sometimes feel disjointed as you jump between different ancestral lines in each generation.

    o **Best For:** A personal genealogical memoir focusing on the research process, or for introducing your immediate ancestry before delving deeper.

3. **Topical Structure:**

    o **How it works:** You organize your family history by themes or topics, rather than strictly by generation or individual.

    o **Examples of Topics:** Migration stories, military service, occupations, religious beliefs, challenges and triumphs, family traditions, life in a specific location (e.g., "Life in the Mining Town," "Farming in the Midwest").

- **Advantages:** Allows you to explore specific aspects of your family's history in depth. It can be particularly engaging for readers interested in specific themes. Allows you to draw connections across different generations and family lines.
- **Disadvantages:** May require more effort to maintain a sense of chronological flow for individual ancestors.
- **Best For:** Highlighting specific interesting aspects of your family history or for shorter narratives focused on a particular theme.

4. **Individual Stories (Biographical Approach):**
    - **How it works:** You focus on telling the life story of one specific ancestor at a time.
    - **Advantages:** Allows you to delve deeply into the details of a single person's life, incorporating information from all the records you've found about them. It can be very engaging as a series of individual portraits.
    - **Disadvantages:** May not provide a strong sense of connection between different individuals and generations unless you explicitly draw those links.
    - **Best For:** Showcasing the lives of particularly interesting or well-documented ancestors, or for creating a collection of biographical sketches.

5. **Geographical Structure:**

- **How it works:** You organize your family history by the locations where your ancestors lived, telling the story of the families who lived in a particular town, county, or region over time.
- **Advantages:** Useful if your research is heavily focused on specific geographical areas. Highlights the connection between your ancestors and the places they inhabited.
- **Disadvantages:** Can be challenging to follow individuals who have moved frequently.
- **Best For:** Family histories with deep roots in a particular locality.

Combining Structures: You don't have to stick to just one structure for your entire family history. You might use a chronological approach for the main narrative of your direct ancestral lines, but include chapters or sections that focus topically on specific themes (such as migration or military service) or feature biographical sketches of fascinating individuals.

Before you start writing, outline your chosen structure. Decide which individuals or family lines you will focus on and how you will organize the information you have gathered about them. A clear structure will make the writing process much more manageable.

Bringing Ancestors to Life: Adding Historical Context and Detail

The difference between a dry recitation of facts and a compelling family history narrative lies in your ability to bring your ancestors to life on the page. This involves going beyond the names, dates, and places to understand the world they inhabited and weave in details that make them relatable human beings.

1. **Research the Historical Context:** For each generation or period you are writing about, research the broader historical context. What were the major political events, social norms, economic conditions, technological advancements, and cultural trends of that time and place? Understanding the world your ancestors lived in is crucial for interpreting their lives.
   - **Examples:** If your ancestors were living in a rural area in the mid-19th century, research agricultural practices, land ownership patterns, and community life in that region. If they were immigrants arriving in a major city, research the conditions in immigrant neighborhoods, the industries they likely worked in, and the challenges they faced.
2. **Incorporate Details from All Your Records:** Don't just rely on vital records and census data. Pull details from all the records you have found:
   - **Land Records:** Describe the land they owned, its size, and its location. What does the legal description tell you about the property?
   - **Probate Records:** What possessions did they own? What will their words reveal about their priorities and relationships? What debts did they have?
   - **Military Records:** What was their experience in the military like? What were the conditions they faced?

- **Newspaper Articles:** What were the local events and news that would have impacted their lives? Were they mentioned in any articles?
- **City Directories:** Where did they live? What businesses were in their neighborhood?
- **Court Records:** Did they have any legal entanglements? What do these records reveal about their interactions with others?

3. **Include Information from Oral Histories:** Weave in the stories, memories, and family lore you gathered from your living relatives. These personal anecdotes provide invaluable color and insight into your ancestors' personalities and experiences. Be sure to indicate when information comes from oral tradition versus documented sources.
4. **Describe Their Environment:** Use historical maps, photographs, and descriptions of the area to help readers visualize where your ancestors lived and worked. Describe their homes, their communities, and the natural landscape.
5. **Explain Their Occupations:** Don't just list an occupation; describe what that job entailed during that time period. What were the working conditions? What skills were required?
6. **Discuss Their Challenges and Triumphs:** Life in the past was often challenging. Write about the difficulties your ancestors faced (poverty, illness, migration, loss) and their resilience in overcoming them. Celebrate their achievements and successes.
7. **Use Descriptive Language:** Employ vivid language and sensory details to bring your narrative to life. Show, don't just tell. Instead of saying "They were

poor," describe the conditions they lived in based on inventory records or historical accounts of poverty in that era.

8. **Emphasize Individuality:** Remember that each ancestor was a unique individual with their own personality, hopes, and dreams. Try to capture their individuality in your writing.

9. **Consider Their Motivations:** Based on the historical context and the records, try to understand *why* your ancestors made the choices they did (e.g., why did they migrate? why did they choose that occupation? why did they move to that specific town?).

Bringing your ancestors to life requires imagination and a deep understanding of the historical context, combined with the specific details you have uncovered in your research. It's about transforming raw data into a compelling human story.

Writing Techniques for Genealogists: Crafting Engaging Prose

Writing a family history narrative is a form of historical writing that also incorporates elements of storytelling. To create an engaging narrative, you need to employ effective writing techniques.

1. **Know Your Audience:** Who are you writing for? If it's primarily for your immediate family, you can assume some shared knowledge. If it's for more distant relatives or a wider audience, you may need to provide more background information.

Tailor your language and level of detail to your intended readers.

2. **Use Clear and Concise Language:** Avoid jargon where possible, or explain it clearly if necessary. Write in a clear, straightforward style that is easy to understand.
3. **Vary Sentence Structure:** Use a mix of short and long sentences to keep your writing interesting and maintain a good rhythm.
4. **Use Transition Words and Phrases:** Use transition words and phrases (e.g., "Meanwhile," "At the same time," "However," "Subsequently") to create smooth connections between sentences and paragraphs and guide the reader through the narrative.
5. **Show, Don't Just Tell:** Instead of simply stating a fact, use descriptive language and details from your research to *show* the reader what life was like for your ancestors.
6. **Maintain a Consistent Point of View:** Decide whether you will write in the first person (e.g., "I discovered that my great-grandmother...") or the third person (e.g., "The researcher discovered that Mary Smith..."). A consistent point of view helps maintain a smooth narrative flow.
7. **Tell Stories within the Story:** Incorporate anecdotes and personal stories from your research and oral histories to illustrate key points and make the narrative more engaging.
8. **Use Dialogue (with Caution):** If you have actual quotes from letters, diaries, or transcribed interviews, you can incorporate dialogue. Be

careful about creating fictional dialogue unless you indicate that it is speculative.
9. **Maintain Accuracy:** While you are telling a story, your narrative must be based on accurate research and documented facts. Do not invent information or embellish details beyond what your research supports. Indicate when something is based on speculation or family lore.
10. **Edit and Proofread Carefully:** Before sharing your work, edit and proofread it thoroughly for grammar, spelling, punctuation, and clarity. Consider asking someone else to read it as well, as they may catch errors you missed.

Writing an engaging family history requires practice, but by focusing on clarity, using descriptive language, and incorporating compelling details, you can craft a narrative that captivates your readers.

Including Visuals: Incorporating Photos, Documents, and Maps

Visuals are a powerful way to enhance your family history narrative and bring your ancestors to life. Incorporating photographs, scanned documents, and maps can make your story more engaging and informative.

1. **Photographs:**
    - **Genealogical Value:** Provide a visual connection to your ancestors. It can reveal clothing styles, hairstyles, and the environment

of the time. Often trigger memories and stories when shared with relatives.
   - **How to Use Them:** Include photographs of your ancestors, their homes, workplaces, or significant locations. Add captions identifying the people in the photo, the date, and the location if known.
   - **Tips:** Digitize your photos at high resolution. Store and organize them carefully (as discussed in Chapter 3). Obtain permission before using photos shared by other family members.
2. **Scanned Documents:**
   - **Genealogical Value:** Provide visual proof of your research findings. It can be fascinating to see the original documents from which your information came. Historical documents often feature interesting visual elements, such as signatures, seals, and handwriting.
   - **How to Use Them:** Include scanned copies of key documents like birth certificates, marriage licenses, census records, deeds, wills, or passenger lists. You don't need to include every document, but select those that are particularly significant or visually interesting.
   - **Tips:** Ensure the scans are clear and legible. Add captions explaining what the document is and its significance. Be mindful of copyright when publishing your work.
3. **Maps:**
   - **Genealogical Value:** Help readers visualize the locations where your ancestors

lived, worked, and migrated. Illustrate geographical connections and migration patterns.

    o **How to Use Them:** Include historical maps of towns, counties, states, or countries relevant to your family history. You can also create simple maps illustrating migration routes or the location of family properties (as discussed in Chapter 9).

    o **Tips:** Ensure maps are clearly labeled and easy to understand. Indicate the period the map represents.

4. **Charts and Diagrams:**

    o **Genealogical Value:** Provide a clear visual overview of family structures and relationships.

    o **How to Use Them:** Include pedigree charts or family group charts, especially for complex family groups or to show direct ancestral lines.

    o **Tips:** Keep charts clear and easy to read. Ensure they are accurate and consistent with your narrative.

General Tips for Including Visuals:

- **Integrate Visuals with the Text:** Place visuals near the relevant sections of your narrative. Refer to the visuals in your text to connect them to the story.
- **Add Captions:** Every visual should have a clear and informative caption.

- **Ensure High Quality:** Use high-resolution scans or photographs so that visuals are clear and easy to see.
- **Consider Copyright:** Be aware of copyright restrictions when using images or documents created by others.
- **Organize Your Visuals:** Keep your digital copies of photos, documents, and maps well-organized in your digital filing system.

Visuals enhance your family history narrative by providing concrete images of your ancestors and the world in which they lived. They make your story more engaging and memorable for your readers.

Citing Sources in Your Writing: Giving Credit and Enabling Verification

Just as you meticulously cited your sources during the research process, it is equally important to cite your sources when you write and share your family history narrative. Proper source citation adds credibility to your work, allows others to verify your findings, and gives credit to the creators and custodians of the records you used.

While you may not need to follow the rigorous academic citation standards for every piece of information in a narrative intended for family, it is essential to provide enough information for readers to understand where your information came from and, if they choose, to find the sources themselves.

Why Cite Sources in Your Writing?

1. **Credibility and Accuracy:** Citations demonstrate that your research is based on evidence and adds to the trustworthiness of your narrative.

2. **Verification:** Allows readers to check your sources and verify the information you present.

3. **Transparency:** Shows the reader the foundation of your conclusions.

4. **Enabling Further Research:** Allows other researchers (including future family members) to build upon your work by easily accessing the sources you used.

5. **Giving Credit:** Acknowledges the individuals and institutions who created and preserved the records.

6. **Avoiding Plagiarism:** It is essential to give credit for information and documents that are not your original work.

How to Cite Sources in Your Writing (Simplified Approach for Beginners):

You can choose a citation style that works for you, but consistency is key. A simple approach for a family history narrative might involve:

- **Endnotes or Footnotes:** Placing numbered citations at the end of each chapter (endnotes) or at the bottom of each page (footnotes). Each citation corresponds to a specific fact or statement in the text.

- **Source List/Bibliography:** Providing a comprehensive list of all the sources you used at the end of the book or narrative.

Information to Include in a Citation (Refer back to Chapter 3 for more detail):

For each source cited, please provide enough information for someone else to locate it. At a minimum, include:

- **Record Type:** (e.g., 1900 U.S. Federal Census, England and Wales Civil Registration Marriage Index, Will of John Smith).
- **Location of the Original Record:** (e.g., National Archives at Washington, D.C., Principal Probate Registry, County Courthouse).
- **Where You Accessed It:** (e.g., Ancestry.com, FamilySearch.org, visited in person).
- **Specific Identifying Information:** (e.g., Census: state, county, enumeration district, sheet number, line number; Will: court, date probated, book and page number; Online Database: database name, image number).

Example of a Simple Footnote/Endnote Citation:

1 1900 U.S. Federal Census, New York, New York County, New York City, Enumeration District 123, Sheet 5A, Household 87, entry for John Smith; accessed via Ancestry.com, image 10 of 30.

2 Will of Thomas Jones, proved 10 July 1855, Carmarthenshire Consistory Court, Public Record

Office, Wales; reference [collection and document number].

3 Marriage Certificate of William Brown and Sarah White, 15 April 1880, Pontypridd Registration District, Glamorgan, Wales; held by [Name of person who has the certificate].

Tips for Citing Sources in Your Writing:

- **Cite as You Write:** It's easiest to add citations as you are writing, rather than trying to go back and add them later.
- **Be Consistent:** Choose one citation style and use it consistently throughout your narrative.
- **Include Enough Detail:** Provide enough information for someone else to find the source.
- **Explain Your Source List:** Briefly explain the purpose of your source list or bibliography at the beginning.
- **Cite Information from Interviews:** When including information from oral histories, cite the interview (e.g., "According to an interview with Aunt Mildred Jones, 15 November 2024").
- **Be Mindful of Privacy for Living Individuals:** When citing sources for information about living relatives, consider the privacy implications and perhaps use more general citations or rely on their consent to share details.

Proper source citation is a mark of a diligent ancestry detective and ensures that your family history narrative is credible, verifiable, and a valuable resource for future generations.

Choosing Your Medium: Books, Websites, Blogs, and Presentations

Once you have written your family history narrative and organized your supporting visuals, you need to decide how you will share your work. There are various mediums available, each with its advantages and disadvantages.

1. **Printed Book:**
   - **Advantages:** A traditional and tangible format that feels substantial and is easy to read. It can be a cherished family heirloom.
   - **Disadvantages:** Can be expensive to print, especially in small quantities or with many photos. Requires significant effort in formatting and layout. Distribution can be challenging.
   - **Options:** Self-publishing through print-on-demand services (like Blurb, Lulu, or Amazon Kindle Direct Publishing) or working with a small local publisher.
2. **Online Family Tree (with narrative features):**
   - **Advantages:** Easily integrates with your genealogical data and tree. Allows you to link sources directly to individuals and facts. Can include photos and scanned documents. Easily shared with family members online. Can be updated easily. Many platforms, including Ancestry, FamilySearch, and MyHeritage, offer this feature.
   - **Disadvantages:** May have limitations on formatting and narrative length compared to a

dedicated book or website. Privacy settings need careful consideration.
- **Options:** Utilize the tree and profile features on major genealogy platforms.

3. **Dedicated Website or Blog:**
    - **Advantages:** Allows for creative design and unlimited content. Can include multimedia elements (videos, audio recordings of interviews). Easily accessible to anyone with internet access. Can be updated regularly.
    - **Disadvantages:** Requires technical skills to set up and maintain (though user-friendly platforms exist). Can have ongoing hosting costs. Consider privacy carefully if you plan to make it public.
    - **Options:** Use website builders (like WordPress, Wix, Squarespace) or blogging platforms (like Blogger, WordPress.com).

4. **Digital Document (PDF, e-book):**
    - **Advantages:** Easy to create and share electronically (via email, cloud storage, or download). Relatively low cost. Can include photos and scanned documents.
    - **Disadvantages:** Less tangible than a printed book. The reading experience can vary depending on the device.
    - **Options:** Save your word processing document as a PDF. Create an e-book using various software or online tools.

5. **Presentations:**
    - **Advantages:** Engaging for a live audience (family gatherings, historical societies). Allows

for storytelling and interaction. Can incorporate visuals and audio.

- **Disadvantages:** Limited audience size. Requires public speaking skills.
- **Options:** Create presentations using software like PowerPoint, Google Slides, or Keynote.

6. **Family Newsletter:**
   - **Advantages:** A good way to share updates on your research periodically with a wider family group. Can be sent electronically or by mail.
   - **Disadvantages:** May be less suitable for sharing a complete, lengthy narrative.

7. **Social Media:**
   - **Advantages:** An Easy way to share snippets of your family history and photos with a broad audience quickly. Can connect you with distant relatives.
   - **Disadvantages:** Not suitable for sharing lengthy narratives or detailed research. Privacy concerns are significant.

Consider your primary audience and your goals when choosing a medium. You might decide to use multiple mediums – perhaps a printed book for close family, an online tree for broader sharing and collaboration, and presentations for family gatherings.

Publishing and Sharing Your Work: Options for Distribution

Once your family history narrative is complete and in your chosen medium, you need to decide how to publish or distribute it to your intended audience.

1. **Self-Publishing (for Books):**
    - **Print-on-Demand (POD):** Services like Blurb, Lulu, and Amazon Kindle Direct Publishing allow you to upload your book file and order copies as needed. This avoids the need for a significant upfront investment in printing. You can often create both print and e-book versions.
    - **Local Printers:** Consider working with a local printing company for a more personalized service, though this may require a larger minimum order.
    - **Formatting and Design:** Self-publishing requires you to handle the formatting, layout, and cover design yourself or hire a designer.
2. **Sharing Online (Websites, Blogs, Digital Documents, Online Trees):**
    - **Private vs. Public:** Decide whether your online family history will be publicly accessible or restricted to invited family members (which is advisable for privacy, especially with information about living individuals).
    - **Sharing Links:** Share links to your website, blog, digital document, or online tree with your family.

- **Collaboration Features:** If using an online tree platform, explore features that allow family members to contribute information or photos.
3. **Direct Distribution (Physical Copies):**
    - **Family Gatherings:** Distribute printed books or digital copies at family reunions or other gatherings.
    - **Mail:** Send copies to family members who live elsewhere.
4. **Depositing in Archives or Libraries:** If your family history has historical significance beyond your immediate family, consider donating copies to local archives, historical societies, or libraries where your ancestors lived. This makes your research accessible to other researchers.
5. **Creating a Family Association or Website:** For larger family groups, establishing a dedicated family association or website can be an effective way to centralize research, share information, and connect with distant relatives.

Tips for Sharing:
- **Start with Close Family:** Share your work with your immediate family first to get their feedback and ensure accuracy, particularly for recent generations.
- **Be Prepared for Different Reactions:** Not everyone in your family may have the same level of interest in genealogy. Be respectful of their interest level.

- **Make it Easy to Access:** Select a sharing method that is straightforward for your intended audience to access and utilize.
- **Encourage Contributions:** Let family members know you welcome their memories, photos, or documents to add to the family history.
- **Be Mindful of Privacy (Again!):** Reiterate the importance of privacy when sharing information, especially about living individuals.

Sharing your family history is a rewarding experience that allows you to connect with your relatives and ensure that your ancestors' stories are remembered and celebrated.

Preserving Your Research for Future Generations: Archiving Your Findings

Your ancestry detective work is a valuable legacy. To ensure that your research, documents, and narrative survive for future generations to access and build upon, it is essential to implement a plan for archiving your findings.

1. **Organize Your Physical Documents:** Continue to organize your physical documents in acid-free folders and boxes, labeled clearly. Store them in a stable environment (cool, dry, away from light).
2. **Organize Your Digital Files:** Maintain a well-organized digital filing system with clear folder

structures and consistent file naming conventions.

3. **Regularly Back Up Your Digital Data:** Implement the 3-2-1 backup rule (three copies, two different media, one offsite copy) for your genealogy software files, digital documents, photos, and written narratives. Use cloud storage and external hard drives.

4. **Create a Master Copy of Your Narrative and Tree:** Save a master copy of your written family history narrative and your genealogy database file (e.g., a GEDCOM file, a standard format for exchanging genealogical data) in a stable, accessible format.

5. **Share Your Research with Multiple Family Members:** Share copies of your research (physical or digital) with several trusted family members who are likely to preserve them. Ensure they understand the organizational system and the importance of the records.

6. **Deposit Copies in Archives or Libraries:** As mentioned earlier, consider depositing copies of your research in relevant archives or libraries, especially if your family has deep roots in a particular area. These institutions are equipped for long-term preservation and make the research accessible to others.

7. **Document Your Organizational System:** Create a document that outlines your physical and digital organizational systems, including file naming conventions and the storage locations

for various types of records. This will help others understand your archive.
8. **Include Information about Your Research Process:** Briefly document how you conducted your research, the sources you used, and any challenges you encountered. This provides context for your findings.
9. **Use Archival-Quality Materials for Physical Copies:** If you create physical copies of your narrative or charts for long-term preservation, use acid-free paper and binders.
10. **Consider Digital Preservation Standards:** For long-term digital preservation, consider saving files in standard, non-proprietary formats (e.g., PDF/A for documents, TIFF or JPEG for images).

Archiving your research is a final act of care for the legacy of your ancestors and the hard work you have put into uncovering their stories. By taking steps to preserve your findings, you ensure that the torch of family history can be passed to future generations.

The Ongoing Journey: Continuing Your Ancestry Adventures

Reaching the point of writing and sharing your family history is a significant accomplishment, but genealogical research is rarely truly "finished." There are always new records being released, new DNA matches to explore, new questions to ask, and new stories to uncover.

Your journey as an ancestry detective is an ongoing adventure. Embrace the fact that there will always be more to discover. Continue to:

- **Explore New Record Sets:** As your experience grows and new records become available online or in archives, continue to search for more information about your ancestors.
- **Connect with New DNA Matches:** As more people test, you will continue to receive new DNA matches. Analyze these matches to find new relatives and potentially uncover new ancestral lines.
- **Revisit Brick Walls:** As you gain more experience and new resources become available, revisit the brick walls in your research. A puzzle that was impossible to solve before might become solvable with new information or techniques.
- **Learn New Skills:** The field of genealogy is constantly evolving. Stay updated on new research techniques, technologies, and historical resources by reading blogs, listening to podcasts, attending webinars, and connecting with other genealogists.
- **Refine and Expand Your Narrative:** As you uncover new information, update and expand your family history narrative.
- **Mentor Other Researchers:** Share your knowledge and experience with others who are starting their genealogical journeys.
- **Enjoy the Process:** Remember why you started this journey in the first place – the

fascinating discovery of your family's past. Continue to enjoy the process of research, analysis, and storytelling.

The stories of your ancestors are waiting to be fully told and shared. You have become a skilled ancestry detective, equipped with the tools and knowledge to uncover the rich tapestry of your family history. By continuing your research, sharing your findings, and preserving your legacy, you ensure that the echoes of the past resonate through the generations to come. Your ancestors' stories are your story – continue the adventure!

More Titles from PAB Publications

Are you concerned about climate change but feel overwhelmed by the science? Do you want to understand the facts and discover actionable solutions for a sustainable future?

Transform Your Parenting Journey and Raise Mindful, Resilient, and Compassionate Children in the Digital Age.

"No Buy Made Easy: A Practical Guide to Sustainable Living and Conscious Choices" is your essential roadmap to breaking free from consumerism and embracing a more fulfilling, affordable, and eco-friendly lifestyle.

Embark on a transformative journey into the heart of meditation and discover the profound pathways to inner peace, self-awareness, and lasting well-being.

Dive into the exhilarating and heart-pounding adventure of "Dolphins of Expedor"! Meet Timothy Shore, a remarkable fourteen-year-old yellow dolphin with the gift of speech, as he is thrust into a perilous whirlpool of destiny to save his cherished underwater city, Expedor, from the brink of annihilation.

Printed in Dunstable, United Kingdom